CONNECT THROUGH EMOTIONAL INTELLIGENCE

WORKBOOK

The companion guide to learn to master self, understand others, and build strong, productive relationships.

Mike Acker

Copyright ©2021, Mike Acker

All rights reserved. No part of this publication may be reproduced, distributed, or transmitted in any form or by any means, including photocopying, recording, or other electronic or mechanical methods, without the prior written permission of the publisher, except in the case of brief quotations embodied in reviews and certain other non-commercial uses permitted by copyright law.

Some names and identifying details have been changed to protect the privacy of individuals.

ISBN: 978-1-954024-28-1

https://www.advantage-publishing.com

To contact, please e-mail: contact@mikeacker.com

TABLE OF CONTENTS

Introduction   1

PART I: ME   **9**
Chapter 1: Know self   10
Chapter 2: Control self   28
Chapter 3: Motivate self   36

PART II: THEM   **51**
Chapter 4: Identify   52
Chapter 5: Empathize   64
Chapter 6: Explore   72

PART III: US   **85**
Chapter 7: Building   86
Chapter 8: Maintaining   103
Chapter 9: Solving   113

About Mike Acker   131

Book Mike Acker   133

NOTE TO THE READER

"A second-rate intellect but a first-rate temperament."

That's how Supreme Court Justice Oliver Wendell Holmes described Franklin D. Roosevelt, the president that led the United States out of the Great Depression and through the Second World War. Likewise, Bill Clinton shared how FDR spoke to his grandfather (and the nation) through his fireside chats in such a way that he believed FDR cared about him personally.

Regardless of what you think of his politics, FDR may not have had the highest IQ but he had an exceptionally high EI—emotional intelligence—and it was that "temperament" that allowed him to carry his country through a very dark time.

The business world is changing. Gone are the days of "bottom line over people." Not necessarily because businesses have suddenly become more altruistic, but they're now recognizing how much people skills affect the bottom line. In every sector, from teaching to manufacturing to law enforcement, brains and brawn no longer cut it. The ability to interact with others—peers, subordinates, and clients—is now non-negotiable.

In Connect through Emotional Intelligence, I outline the essential role that Emotional Intelligence plays for success at every level of your life. I also talk about the ways it helps establish both interpersonal wellbeing (how we relate to ourselves) and intrapersonal wellbeing (how we relate to one another).

While some are naturally more gifted in the areas of understanding and controlling emotions, or in empathizing and connecting with others, we all have room for improvement. But we're not going to get there simply by reading. We need to dig in and do the work. That's where this interactive workbook comes in.

This workbook is a companion to Connect through Emotional Intelligence, designed specifically to help you take that content and apply it to your own life for individual growth. While some of the content from Connect through Emotional Intelligence will be included throughout this book, the exercises in this book are only found here. They'll help you move from reflection to real-world practice. In time, it will produce genuine growth and improvement in your Emotional Intelligence.

These exercises are designed to be used in conjunction with the Connect through Emotional Intelligence book. I recommend you read a chapter from Connect through Emotional Intelligence first, then turn to the corresponding chapter in this workbook. These exercises will ask a lot of you. They will ask you to be honest with yourself. They will push you to commit to creating practical plans. They will ask you to apply what you're learning toward both interpersonal and intrapersonal health.

As with anything that involves change, you're likely to feel some reluctance along the way. That's okay. In fact, that's to be expected. When you do, notice your resistance, make a note of why you're feeling it, and then do your best to set that response aside and keep going. We all have reservations when it comes to doing something that stretches us. That will certainly be true here.

Maybe your hesitation will arise when it comes to locating the source of your emotions—you're afraid of what you'll find. Or, maybe you'll realize that you don't want to empathize with certain people! Don't feel guilty about any of that. Be curious, not judgmental. Notice it, make a note of it, but don't let it get in the way of your genuine growth and greater health!

And, don't forget: you're not alone. We all have room for improvement. We're all here because we're looking to do better. We're all in this together.

So, let's get started.

Mike Acker

Important note: Improving your Emotional Intelligence requires courage, and some aspects of this book may push you further emotionally than you'd like. Please understand that I am not a counselor and this workbook is not a substitute for professional advice. If anything here begins to feel unsafe, please set it aside and consult a mental health professional.

INTRODUCTION

WHAT IS EMOTIONAL INTELLIGENCE?

IQ is all about your brain—EI is about your heart. Said another way, EI represents your relative ability to make sound judgements about your emotions and the emotions of others and then it will help you choose the wisest course of action. It doesn't just impact your personal life. Historically, we've tended to focus on IQ, but research shows that academic intelligence is responsible for predicting only about 20 percent of someone's success.[1] More and more, the business world is recognizing how important EI is and has begun making hiring and firing decisions based on it. The good news is that, unlike IQ, everyone has the ability to vastly improve their EI. It takes work, but it is possible.

From Connect Through Emotional Intelligence, page 13

Have you ever known someone who was incredibly bright or exceptionally gifted and just killed it when they worked alone, but working with or—worse yet—for them was a nightmare? Another example: Have you ever watched Big Bang Theory? The show's whole "brilliant but socially awkward" trope is based on the fact that someone can have a very high IQ but seem almost incapable of cultivating healthy interactions with others. It makes for hilarious gags but is no joke in real life.

Taking the extra step to purchase this workbook demonstrates that you are committed to improving your EI. What do you hope to gain from this journey?

_____
_____
_____
_____
_____
_____
_____
_____

---

1   Goleman, Emotional Intelligence, 34.

I truly believe you can do that. But it will take hard work—change always does. Take a moment to record why this matters to you. Reflect back on this when you want to quit partway through.

_____
_____
_____
_____
_____
_____
_____
_____

HOW'S YOUR EI?

First things first—how is your EI? What is your starting point? There are many online assessments of varying quality. Perhaps the best one is the Mayer-Salovey-Caruso Emotional Intelligence Test (MSCEIT), but it requires working with a certified presenter. Instead, use these questions for a self-assessment:

How to Complete:
1. For each question, give yourself a 2 if you view the area as strength for you, a 1 if it's something you are moderately skilled at, and a 0 if it's an area that's challenging for you.
2. Use the lines provided to complete qualitative self assesment/explain your score.

How "in touch" are you with your emotions?

_____
_____

How easily can you figure out why you feel what you feel?

_____
_____

Do you understand and appreciate both your strengths and weaknesses?

_____
_____

How long does it take for you to recover from a distressing emotion?

_____
_____

How easily are you able to adapt to changes?

_____
_____

Can you sense how other people are feeling and understand their point of view?

_____
_____

How are you at negotiating conflict?

_____
_____

How well do you work on a team?

_____
_____

Self-assessment Total
Tally your previous answers to rank your current EI on scale of 1-16.

Don't take it personally, but we're all quite apt at self-deceit. Plus, EI is as much about how you interact with others as how you handle your emotions. For that reason, there's no substitute for getting external input. This is a big step, but I want you to find two people that you trust to give honest feedback, one who knows you personally and the other professionally, and ask them to complete this assessment on your behalf (you can find printable PDFs of these questions at content.mikeacker.com).

Personal:

How "in touch" are they with their emotions?

_____
_____

How easily can they figure out why they feel what they feel?

_____
_____

Do they understand and appreciate both their strengths and weaknesses?

_____
_____

How long does it take for them to recover from a distressing emotion?

_____
_____

How easily are they able to adapt to changes?

_____
_____

Can they sense how other people are feeling and understand their point of view?

_____
_____

How are they at negotiating conflict?

_____
_____

How well do they work on a team?

_____
_____

Personal assessment Total
Tally your previous answers to rank _____'s current EI on scale of 1-16.

Other Notes and Feedback
Do you have another other comments or feedback about _____'s current EI?

_____
_____
_____
_____
_____
_____
_____
_____

Professional:

How "in touch" are they with their emotions?

_____
_____

How easily can they figure out why they feel what they feel?

_____
_____

Do they understand and appreciate both their strengths and weaknesses?

_____
_____

How long does it take for them to recover from a distressing emotion?

_____
_____

How easily are they able to adapt to changes?

_____
_____

Can they sense how other people are feeling and understand their point of view?

_____
_____

How are they at negotiating conflict?

_____
_____

How well do they work on a team?

_____
_____

Professional assessment Total
Tally your previous answers to rank _____'s current EI on scale of 1-16.

Other Notes and Feedback
Do you have another other comments or feedback about _____'s current EI?

_____
_____
_____
_____
_____
_____
_____
_____
_____
_____
_____

Read through your own responses and the responses you requested from someone close to you. Are there any surprises? Did you learn anything new about yourself?

_____
_____
_____
_____
_____

Not that we have a starting point, let's begin this journey!

From Connect Through Emotional Intelligence, page 21

Imagine that you and a bunch of friends are planning a week-long camping trip the next state over, involving about a dozen cars. Vehicle-wise, there are three key components for a safe journey:
1. *You need to make sure that your car is running well and is capable of making the trip.*
2. *Once you're on the road, you need to interact safely with countless vehicles, watching for brake lights and anticipating erratic driving.*
3. *You need to coordinate with your friends to arrive at the same location.*

...So, the three parts of the book are:

01	02	03
ME Understanding and controlling my own "car."	**THEM** Being able to read and safely interact with the other "cars."	**US** Interacting with the other "cars" in my group to arrive at our desired destination.

PART I:

ME

Chapter 1: KNOW SELF

From Connect Through Emotional Intelligence, page 28

Healthy Emotional Intelligence starts with self. Returning to the car analogy, you need to make sure that your car is in good working condition before taking it out on the road. That's the focus of Part One. In this chapter, we'll focus on self-awareness—discovering what's under the hood.

Self-awareness is hard. Many people don't recognize how they come across to others. They're unable to name their strongest attributes, unaware of how their communication style affects others and struggle with knowing and naming what they're feeling. But lack of self-awareness has the potential to damage our work friendships, relationships, and romantic relationships.

If knowing yourself is the beginning of wisdom, as Aristotle says, it's also the beginning of Emotional Intelligence.

GETTING TO KNOW YOURSELF

Before others can recognize your gifts, you must first recognize them in yourself. Having a high EI requires knowing yourself.

How well would you say you know yourself? Many of us think we do—until we're put on the spot.

What is your favorite trait about yourself?

_____

_____

What is your least favorite personal trait?

_____

_____

What do you want others to notice about you?

_____
_____

What do you think others actually notice?

_____
_____

How do others feel in your presence?

_____
_____

Now, which of these questions were the easiest to answer? What was the most challenging? Looking back over your responses, is there anything that made you pause? If so, what?

_____
_____
_____
_____
_____
_____
_____
_____
_____
_____
_____

CONFIDENCE

How well-rooted is your sense of self? For some of us, it's so strong that we remain unwavering in our self-understanding no matter what others say about us—even to a fault. For others, our sense of self is much more transitory, easily shaped by what others say or how they treat us.

Insecurity and bravado are equally destructive to developing a high EI. Knowing yourself requires a strong, yet accurate self-confidence, and that is the goal of this section.

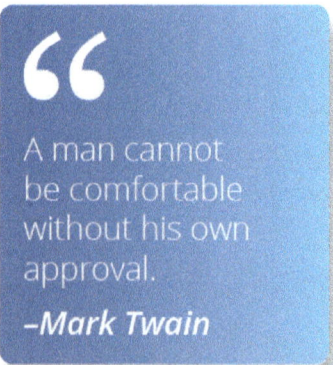

> A man cannot be comfortable without his own approval.
> –Mark Twain

Confidence Changes Over Time

Research shows that self-confidence isn't static; it changes over time. In a longitudinal study of more than 164,000 participants (roughly split equally between men and women), confidence generally increased until the age of 60 or 70. Then, it faced a dramatic decline.[1]

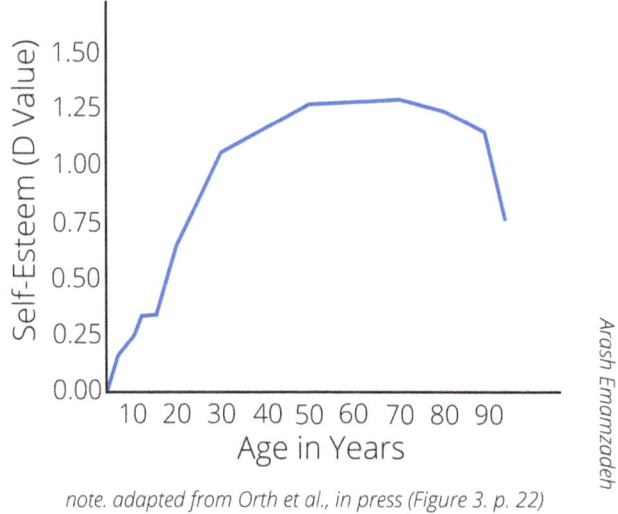

Estimated Self-Esteem Changes from 4-94

note. adapted from Orth et al., in press (Figure 3. p. 22)

Of course, this represents the average and significant life experiences that can affect our confidence, for better and for worse. Early adolescence is a common low point for confidence—no surprise there! But then, it typically picks up around the time most of us got our driver's license and gained a sense of independence. In adulthood, confidence tends to increase more quickly in early adulthood, then levels out as we approach 60

---

[1] Arash Emamzadeh, Psychology Today, "How Self-Esteem Changes Between the Ages of 4 and 94," https://www.psychologytoday.com/us/blog/finding-new-home/201809/how-self-esteem-changes-between-the-ages-4-and-94

years old. This increase in confidence is the result of a steady growth in our personality traits. As noted in Psychology Today:

> "...development during adulthood is directed toward improvement on personality traits (emotional stability, conscientiousness, and agreeableness) associated with those social roles (e.g., as an employee, spouse, parent). Therefore, given that improvement on these personality traits is associated with greater self-esteem ... people generally experience improved self-esteem throughout adulthood."[1]

These general trends in confidence over time can be helpful for recognizing our own changes and preparing for the future.

Reflecting on your own life, how has your confidence changed over time? Has it steadily increased, or has it involved more peaks and valleys over the years?

When would you say your confidence was at its highest? What were the reason(s) for that?

_____
_____
_____
_____
_____

When has your confidence been at its lowest? What do you think caused that?

_____
_____
_____
_____
_____

---

[1] Arash Emamzadeh, Psychology Today, "How Self-Esteem Changes Between the Ages of 4 and 94," https://www.psychologytoday.com/us/blog/finding-new-home/201809/how-self-esteem-changes-between-the-ages-4-and-94

Ch. 1 Know Self

Areas of Insecurity

This might be uncomfortable, but let's spend some time examining those areas where you feel least self-confident.

When was a time you felt embarrassed by something about yourself? What happened?

_____
_____
_____
_____
_____
_____
_____
_____
_____
_____
_____
_____
_____
_____
_____
_____
_____

I'm genuinely sorry that happened. Embarrassment—as well as its cousin, shame—can be devastating. The impacts of an embarrassing experience like that can be long-lasting. But, we're going to work on it together.

What aspect of yourself have you been embarrassed by? Was it a physical trait? Something you said or did? Something about your personality? Whatever it was, try to locate the source of this embarrassment. Be as specific as possible.

_____
_____
_____
_____
_____
_____
_____

Naming your embarrassment and its source is hard but growing in confidence requires coming to terms with these things rather than letting them silently affect you. We all have areas of growth and improvement, but no one deserves to live with long-lasting shame.

So, how do you feel about this part of yourself today? Are you still embarrassed about it? Or, are you now more confident?

_____
_____
_____
_____
_____
_____
_____

If you still have room for improvement here, that's okay. Now that you've named it, make a point of returning to this question—one month, six months, and one year from now—and checking in with yourself. Are you seeing improvement? Often, we don't recognize growth in our day-to-day experience, but, over time, we can see how far we've come.

One more thing: In my book *Speak With No Fear*, I talk about the difference between wounds and scars. You'd be surprised how many people are held back from success in public speaking because of past wounds and embarrassments! Unless it is treated, a wound only becomes more painful over time. That to say, if your past embarrassments still feel like an open wound, consider working with a mental health professional to treat them—doing so has been a life-changer for me!

Areas of Strength

These next exercises should be more fun—let's focus on your strengths!

What three personal traits are you most proud of? What do you enjoy about being you?

01 _____

02 _____

03 _____

💡 **Applied EI:** Now that you've identified your top three favorite personal traits, find a way to remind yourself of them every day. Write them down on a sticky note and put it on your bathroom mirror or take a picture and make it the background on your phone. Make sure you see it every day.

This just isn't a feel-good exercise. Confidence and excelling in life require building on your strengths. If you struggled to complete this exercise, I'd recommend taking the CliftonStrengths assessment. Understanding and honing your best traits is a gamechanger!

What is your proudest accomplishment, the thing you want other people to know about you?

_____
_____
_____
_____

Well done! I bet that took a lot of hard work and commitment. Reminding yourself of things like that is a great way to instill confidence for future challenges.

Next, we're going to move into another important aspect of knowing yourself: being able to name your emotions.

NAME THE EMOTION

How many emotions can you name? Research shows that humans are capable of a myriad of emotions, but most of us have trouble naming more than 10. Take a minute—literally, 60 seconds—to write down as many emotions as you can. Ready? Go!

_____
_____
_____
_____
_____
_____
_____
_____

How'd you do? Were you able to name more than 10? How about 20? If you could, you're already excelling!

Naming emotions in general is one thing. How good are you at recognizing what you're feeling in the moment of an emotional response? Knowing yourself starts with:
- Recognizing your emotions when you feel them,
- Tracing your emotions back to their source, and
- Controlling your emotions, before they control you.

We'll start with some exercises to practice recognizing and naming your emotions when you are experiencing them. This is harder than it sounds.

Being emotionally aware is key to having a high EI. It begins with recognizing your own emotions. You must be able to literally name them. The trouble is, we have a lot of different emotions, and they can be hard to distinguish at times.

One tool for naming the particular emotion you're experiencing is to recognize the general one, then narrow it down from there.

Ch. 1 Know Self

Many of us can name our emotions in broad terms, but we struggle to get beyond basic labels such as "Happy," "Sad," "Angry," or "Frustrated." The Plutchik Wheel of Emotions, developed by American Psychologist, Dr. Robert Plutchik, is an incredibly useful tool for this. He spent years studying and categorizing our emotional experiences, and he determined that we have eight basic emotions (starting from the top of the next circle after the center): joy, trust, fear, surprise, sadness, disgust, anger, and anticipation.

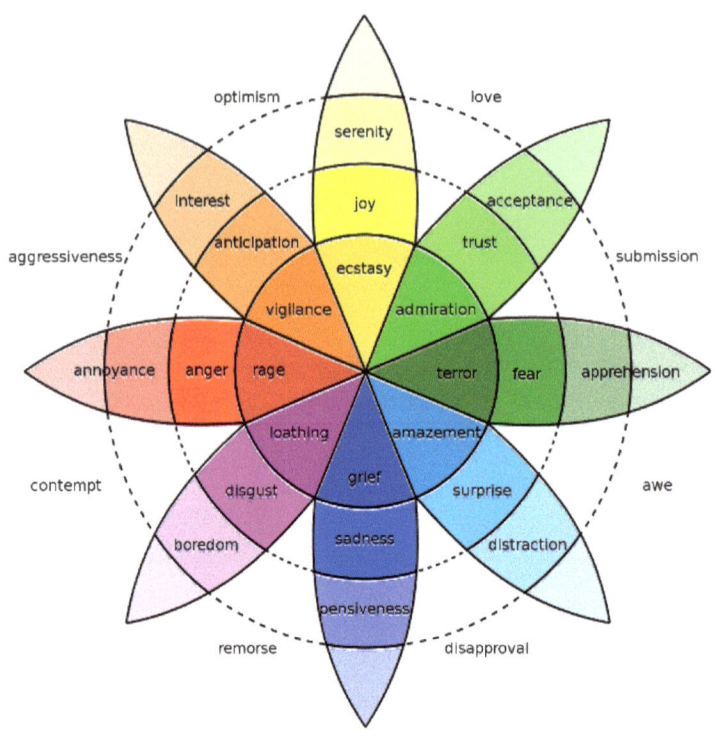

Figure 2: The Plutchik Wheel of Emotions

Notice that all the primary emotions are paired with the opposing one on the opposite side of the circle. For example, the opposite of joy is sadness. And the opposite of anger is fear. Dr. Plutchik's research showed that human emotions are much, much more complex than we think and they are interrelated. Being able to visualize these relationships can help us narrow down our feelings and name them as specifically as possible.

The Intensity Scale

Here's something else to point out about the Emotion Wheel. Did you notice that the colors of the emotions are darker toward the center? That's intentional. If you follow the emotions from the outermost circle to the center of the Wheel, they increase in intensity. Moving inward, annoyance is followed by anger and then rage.

Ch. 1 Know Self

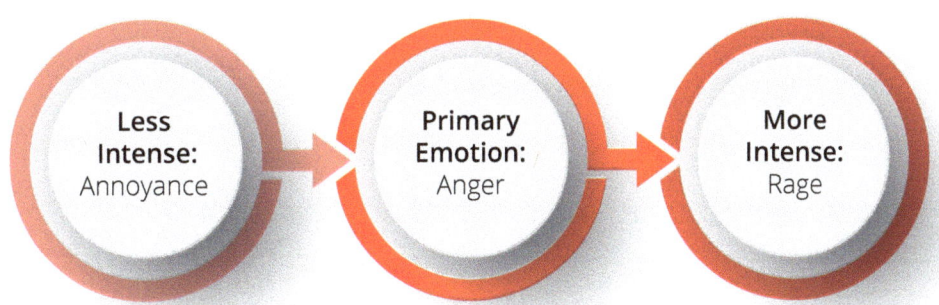

Understanding and using this scale of intensity can also be helpful for naming our emotions. When you locate what you're feeling, check with its neighbors to see if you're feeling a more or less intense emotion than you initially thought. Maybe, for example, you assumed you're feeling sad. After checking in, you may realize what you're really dealing with is grief.

Combining Emotions

If you take another look at the Wheel of Emotions, you'll notice that there are also words that aren't colored: love, submission, awe, disapproval, remorse, contempt, aggressiveness, and optimism. These emotions are a combination of two of the Primary Emotions. Love, for example, comes from a combination of joy and trust. Contempt comes from a combination of anger and disgust. Emotions are connected to one another in a web of intricate relationships, increasing and decreasing in intensity, and combining to create another emotion entirely.

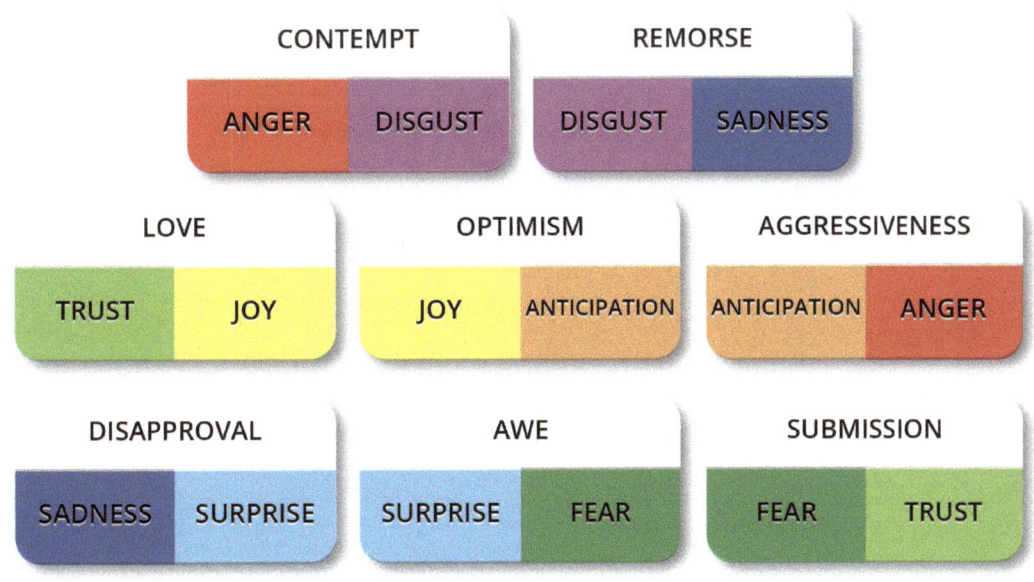

Thinking of these combinations as the intersection of two other emotions can be another helpful way to understand and name what you're feeling. The way to better understand your emotions is to become aware of how they are related to each other.

Study the chart above and observe the connections. What combinations surprises you the most? What do these connections teach you about emotions?

_____
_____
_____
_____
_____
_____
_____
_____

Exercise: Test Your Knowledge of Emotion Combinations

Match the combination on the left with the resulting emotion from the right-hand column. (No peeking!)

What emotion is produced by:

1. Surprise and Fear? _____   A. Love

2. Anticipation and Anger? _____   B. Disapproval

3. Trust and Joy? _____   C. Contempt

4. Anger and Disgust? _____   D. Awe

5. Fear and Trust? _____   E. Submissiveness

6. Sadness and Surprise? _____   F. Optimism

7. Disgust and Sadness? _____   G. Agressiveness

8. Joy and Anticipation? _____   H. Remorse

How'd you do? Were you able to get four or more right on your own? Five or more? Six? If you were able to identify 50 percent or more of these combinations, great job! If not, study the ones you missed and give it another shot. The better you are at identifying these combinations of emotions, the better you will understand how they relate to one another.

Tools like The Plutchik Wheel of Emotions can help us:
- move from broad categories to more specific labels,
- become more self-aware and self-compassionate, and
- improve our ability to share how we're feeling with others.

> "Feelings do not manifest themselves in isolation.
>
> –Dr. Robert Plutchnik"

Exercise: Get Specific

Let's put this study into practice. What was an intense emotional experience from your past week? Write it down, including the surrounding details:

_____
_____
_____
_____
_____
_____
_____
_____
_____
_____
_____
_____
_____

Good. Clearly there was something that stood out to you. Something that had an emotional impact. Now, name the emotion you experienced without using any tools:

_____

Now, go back and find the closest emotion using the Plutchik Wheel and look at the surrounding emotions. How does this help you better understand how you felt?

___

💡 **Applied EI:** For the next week, write down an emotion when you're feeling it and then bring it to the Emotion Wheel when you have time. Look at its neighbors, and then look at the intersection of the Primary Emotions. Get as specific as possible in naming what you felt.

As you use these tools more and more, you will find that you are better able to identify the specific emotion you're experiencing, when you're experiencing them. And, as we will see, you have to get specific before you can begin to address that emotion. But it all starts with being able to name it.

FIND THE SOURCE

Ever had a stomach ache and had trouble figuring out why? Maybe those week-old leftovers should have been thrown out after all. Or, maybe your stomach doesn't like curry as much as you do! Either way, the rumbling in your stomach wasn't a coincidence. Likewise, how we feel is always caused by something. But discovering that source takes time, work, and practice.

Identifying your emotions requires going past the surface, beyond your actions, and what you can see. A trained professional can sometimes be helpful, even necessary. In my case, I needed a professional to help identify the complexity of what I was feeling during an especially significant life transition. Maybe you do, too. When we have had that help, we are better equipped to open the hood and identify the specific emotion we're experiencing in a stressful situation.

During a difficult experience, don't get so distracted by your actions that you lose sight of what's going on under the hood. And don't guess. Do the work. Dig in. And, if you need to, find someone who can help. You'll be grateful for the tools you'll receive when things break down.

Now that we've practiced identifying emotions, we're ready to roll up our sleeves and dig deeper to find the source. There will be opportunities to revisit experiences that caused a strong emotional response, but if you ever don't feel comfortable doing so, just skip it for now

EXERCISE: TRACING THE SOURCE

For the next week, I want you to check in with yourself at the end of each day. Mark when you felt the following emotions in the left column. Then, do your best to identify its source and write that down in the right column.

You'll notice that the Primary Emotions are in Bold, with their associated emotions in the rows directly above and below them. You'll also notice the shading of each box increasing in intensity, as the emotion increases. The Combination Emotion will appear in the unshaded box, between the two neighboring Primary Emotions.

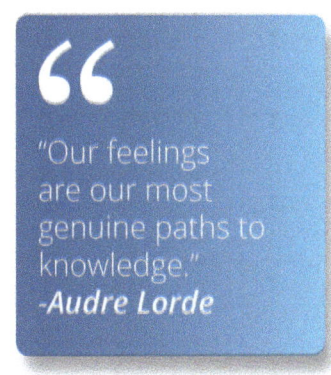

"Our feelings are our most genuine paths to knowledge."
-Audre Lorde

Emotion: Source:

Serenity	
Joy	
Ecstasy	
Love	

Emotion: Source:

Acceptance	
Trust	
Admiration	
Submission	

Emotion: Source:

Apprehension	
Fear	
Terror	
Awe	

Emotion: Source:

Distraction	
Surprise	
Amazement	
Disapproval	

Emotion: Source:

Pensiveness	
Sadness	
Grief	
Remorse	

Emotion: Source:

Boredom	
Disgust	
Loathing	
Contempt	

Emotion: Source:

Annoyance	
Anger	
Rage	
Aggressiveness	

Emotion: Source:

Interest	
Anticipation	
Vigilance	
Optimism	

Pairing our emotions with their source is usually easier in hindsight—usually but not always. Or sometimes, you'll identify a source that's actually just the surface cause, but there's a deeper one you're missing. One key indicator of deeper causes is disproportionality—if the intensity of your emotional response seems disproportional to the source cause, then there's probably something deeper. Choose one or two disproportional emotions and sources from above and take the time to try to identify the deeper cause.

Emotion: _____

_____
_____
_____
_____
_____
_____
_____
_____
_____

Emotion: _____

_____
_____
_____
_____
_____
_____
_____
_____
_____

At the end of the week, take some time to evaluate how this exercise went. On a scale of 1 to 10 (1: Easiest, 10: Most Difficult), rate how hard it was to identify your emotions and their source:

1   2   3   4   5   6   7   8   9   10

What do you think this says about the current state of your Emotional Intelligence?

_____
_____
_____
_____
_____
_____
_____
_____
_____
_____

> "Sometimes you feel like you're on fire and you don't even know where it burns."
> -Audrey Assad

By taking the time to study past emotions and tracing them back to their source, you'll improve your ability to do so in "real time." And the good news is that it gets easier with practice!

Applied EI: For the next week, keep note of when you're feeling a strong emotion. As quickly as possible, locate its source. At the end of the week, rate your success on the same 1 to 10 scale:

1   2   3   4   5   6   7   8   9   10

How did your response compare after a week of practice? Are you finding it easier to locate the source of your emotions compared to when you started?

The more you stick with this practice, the more second-nature it will become, and the greater your EI will be!

Chapter 2:
CONTROL SELF

You've probably seen slapstick comedies where a steering wheel comes off in the driver's hands. But in reality, I can think of few things more frightening than driving through a mountain pass and having the steering wheel fall off. That's an apt description of a person with low EI—trying to navigate tricky roads with a revving engine of emotion but no ability to control it. Self-control is about far more than not binging at the buffet. The mark of high EI is the ability to steer your emotions.

"They *made* me angry." Have you ever found yourself saying that? Or heard someone else say it? It's a pretty common phrase, right? The problem is, it's not true. No one makes you feel angry. In fact, no one makes you feel *anything*. Your response to any situation is your responsibility. Those with a high EI know that they are always in control of their emotions, no matter the situation. Like those who succeed in other areas of life, those with a high EI have a high level of self-control, specifically over their emotions.

Self-Control Assessment:

On a scale from 1 to 10, where 1 is the least self-controlled, and 10 is the highest, how are you at controlling your emotions and emotional responses?

Routine-Oriented   Spontaneity

1   2   3   4   5   6   7   8   9   10

Tell me more. Why that score?

_____

_____

_____

_____

If you scored lower on the assessment:

Our ability to control our emotions is affected by many factors, such as our temperament, the examples we saw in our childhood, and our stress level. What are some of the factors that may make self-control more difficult for you?

_____
_____
_____
_____

What are some practical things you can do to overcome those obstacles?

_____
_____
_____
_____

If you scored high on the assessment:

Sometimes "too much" emotional self-control is the result of being emotionally repressed (think of Spock's character on Star Trek). Do you tend to hold in your emotions or direct them in a healthy way? Why do you give that answer?

_____
_____
_____
_____
_____
_____
_____
_____

CONTROL YOUR EMOTIONS BEFORE THEY CONTROL YOU

The first part of controlling our emotions—before they control us—involves naming them and locating their source, which we worked on in the last chapter.

From Connect Through Emotional Intelligence, page 41

If we have a low EI, however, whatever emotion arises has the power to overwhelm us, whether it's disappointment, anger, or nervousness. For example, let's say you're in the middle of a stressful work situation when your child asks for help. If you erupt with, "Get out of here!", that's a sign of low EI. When emotions from one situation spill into another, without any control, that's a sure sign that you're in need of help. When people react like that, they often say, "I can't control myself." But that's not true—they probably wouldn't yell, "Get out of here!" to their boss. And even if they lack control in the moment, it's still possible to build self-control when the pressure isn't on; therefore, improving their ability to handle future high-stress moments.

You may not be running against the world's fastest sprinters in the next Summer Olympics, no matter how disciplined you are, but that doesn't mean you can't perform at the highest level of EI. It takes work and it requires self-control, but it's just as possible for you as it is for anyone else. That's what we're aiming for: controlling our emotions before they control us.

Next comes taking proactive steps to create a buffer between that source and your response. Here are some helpful exercises to do just that.

>
> "You learned to run from what you feel, and that's why you have nightmares.
> To deny is to invite madness. To accept is to control."
>
> - Megan Chance, The Spiritualist

EXERCISE: TAKE A BREATH

How's your breathing? At this moment, it's probably at rest. But the moment you feel excited, afraid, or agitated, your body will experience a physical response. Your heart rate will spike. Your hands may become sweaty. And your breathing will quicken. Under enough stress, you will struggle to breathe deep and get enough oxygen.

Before your emotions get away from you, do this: intentionally focus on your breathing. This practice will help you regain a sense of peace and gain control over your emotions, before you respond.

Ch. 2 Control Self

Let's practice now—before you're in the middle of a stressful situation!

For a 50-count, close your eyes and pay attention to your breathing. Feel your breath enter your body through your nose. Then, as you breathe out through your mouth, focus on your breath leaving your body, and count "1." Continue this practice, counting each out-breath, until you count all the way up to 50.

How did that feel? Was it easy or difficult? Where did your thoughts go during this exercise?

_____
_____
_____
_____
_____
_____

Do you feel more relaxed now? If yes, try to explain in what way and where in your body you feel the relaxation.

_____
_____
_____
_____
_____
_____

♀Applied EI: If you found this exercise helpful, what is one way you could introduce this practice into your daily routine? Before hopping onto your email in the morning? Before crawling into bed at night? Write down the time that will work best for you:

_____
_____

Commit to this breathing exercise for one week and see how you feel. You may just decide to keep it going!

PAUSE FOR POWER

We can all react in ways we regret. Maybe you're on a call when your daughter barges into the room asking if you've seen her favorite stuffed animal. Or maybe you're practicing for an upcoming presentation when the power goes out. In each of these scenarios, we are tempted to respond with frustration, impatience, and anger. And when that happens, that's when we're likely to act in a way that we'll regret.

From Connect Through Emotional Intelligence, page 45

When you're overwhelmed or angry, you're likely to become "flooded." This means more than being hit by a flood of emotions. On a physiological level, our amygdala will put our body into "fight, flight, or freeze." It will shut down the part of our brain responsible for reasoning. No matter how logical of a person you may think you are, when you're flooded, you are literally incapable of thinking clearly—and men are more prone to this effect than women. You cannot reason your way past being flooded. Deep breaths help, but your body needs at least twenty minutes to reset.

This is a crucial aspect of EI—being able to regulate and control yourself, instead of allowing the situation to control you. When you're feeling overwhelmed, wait until you have regained self-control before responding. Pause, center yourself, and then respond—not the other way around.

Now that you've experienced the difference pausing-to-focus-on-your-breathing can make, the next step is to do it when you're feeling overwhelmed and are tempted to give up control of your emotions. But that's just the start of an Emotionally Intelligent response. Let's try an exercise to take this practice even further.

EXERCISE: ENVISION THE AFTERMATH

Can you think of a time when you "lost control" of your emotions and acted in a way that you later regretted? Who was involved? What happened that led to your response? Write it down now:

_____

_____

_____

Next, I'd like you to envision a different response. Let's try that now. What might have happened if you took 10 seconds to focus on your breathing, before responding? How might things have played out?

_____
_____
_____
_____
_____
_____

Going beyond taking time to focus on your breathing and calming your mind before responding, taking the time to imagine the consequences of your response can vastly improve the outcome. That means envisioning the aftermath of not controlling your emotions. We all know that saying "I didn't mean to say/do that" won't eliminate the damage.

From Connect Through Emotional Intelligence, page 48

It wasn't until later, after I had calmed down and got some perspective, that I realized how rude I'd been. I took out my domestic frustrations on him. Returning to the driving metaphor, my car had been out of control and I'd run over him. I tried to apologize, but the damage was done. The relationship never returned to what it had been—all because I didn't pause to envision the aftermath.

Imagine an emotionally charged conversation that you are likely to have in the near future. What are some of the ways that an uncontrolled response from you could do long-term damage? Be as specific as possible.

_____
_____
_____
_____
_____
_____

Now let's imagine three more positive alternatives and how they would create a better outcome.

From Connect Through Emotional Intelligence, page 49

Starting with curiosity rather than anger will improve your relationships and your work. It will also improve your emotional wellbeing and grow your EI.

Curiosity: Trying to understand the other person's perspective

_____
_____
_____
_____

Gratitude: Looking for something of value in the other person's perspective

_____
_____
_____
_____

Humor: Prevents mole hills from becoming mountains (note: do not use humor when it really is a mountain).

_____
_____
_____
_____

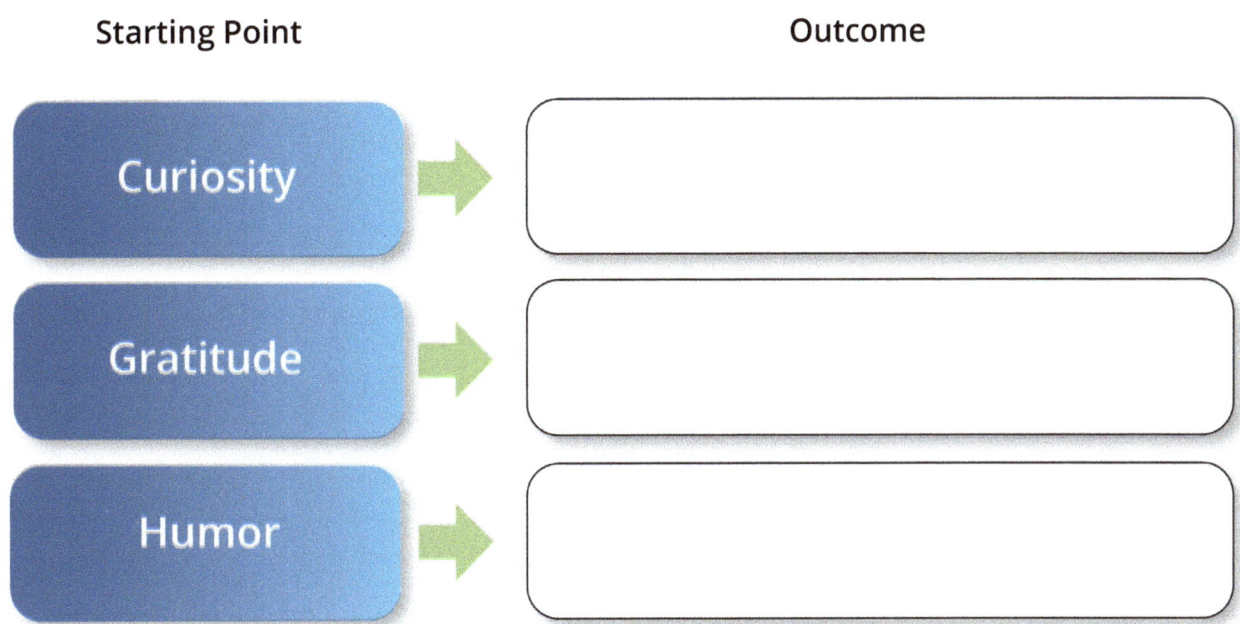

Great work! Curiosity, gratitude, and humor can all be potentially helpful ways of reframing our response for a more positive outcome.

When our emotions are running high, we can feel like we have no other options but to respond in a particular way—with anger, impatience, or frustration, for example. The truth is, we always have more options than we think we do at the moment. We simply need more space to imagine other possibilities.

As you're imagining yourself reacting differently to this same situation, you're proactively training your brain for alternative ways of responding. The more you practice this imaginative exercise of Envisioning the Aftermath in advance, the more likely you'll respond better in the future.

> 💡 **Applied EI:** This next week, take note of anytime you feel tempted to give up control of your emotions. As soon as that happens, focus on your breathing for 10 seconds—count silently, if you need to.

While you're counting, imagine the outcome of the various possible responses. Make sure you've regained control, so that you can respond for the best possible outcome.

Remember, this may feel awkward, artificial, or even inappropriate at first. That's okay. It's better than reacting out of control. And, the more you pause for control, focus on your breathing, and envision the aftermath, the easier it will be to respond with Emotional Intelligence. Each time, you're growing and improving. Keep up the great work!

Chapter 3: MOTIVATE SELF

If our emotions are the engine that power us, and if self-control and self-regulation are the steering wheel and brakes, then this chapter is about the gas pedal. Sure, you can go all Spock and repress your emotions, but that's like ripping the accelerator out of your car. It might be a lot safer to never leave the driveway, but you'll never get anywhere either. That to say, having a high EI means understanding what motivates us and using our emotions to take us where we want to go.

Emotions aren't simply meant to be controlled—they're meant to be harnessed
They can drive us to accomplish great things, if intentionally directed. That's why self-motivation is a key area of Emotional Intelligence. Those with a high EI are driven by a deeply rooted motivation that helps us overcome obstacles that arise and threaten to throw us off course.

If knowing yourself is the beginning of wisdom, as Aristotle says, it's also the beginning of Emotional Intelligence.

Those with a high EI live by design. They are driven by a sense of purpose and meaning, which gives them internal motivation. These people are better equipped to respond to challenges that arise because they have a long-term sense of where they are going, and they know why they are heading there. When we live without design, we steer toward our default patterns. Without intentionality, we will get stuck in a rut with our work, finances, health, time, speech, and relationships—and ruts can't ever take you somewhere new.
Yes, some people are more self-motivated than others. But motivation, like many things, can be built up and developed.

Some of us excel in self-motivation and others of us struggle—always needing some sort of external pressure. We're going to spend some time focusing on your internal motivation, and how we can work together to improve it.

MOTIVATION SELF-ASSESSMENT

On a scale of 1 to 10, where one is the least motivated and 10 is the most, how internally motivated are you?

1 2 3 4 5 6 7 8 9 10

Why did you give yourself this score? How could it be higher?

_____
_____
_____
_____
_____
_____

We all learn by others' example—for better and for worse! Noticing someone else's habits can improve our own motivation. Who are some people in your life who live with a high degree of self-motivation? Maybe it's a friend, family member, or colleague. Write down their names:

_____
_____

What are some ways that you would like to model your own motivation on this person?

_____
_____
_____
_____
_____

REASONS: FIND YOUR PASSIONS

What drives you? What gets you up each morning and makes you look forward to your day? In 2015, Andrew Rea struggled to get out of bed and sunk into depression. But today, his YouTube channel, "Binging With Babish," where he combines his passions for cooking and filmmaking by recreating recipes from familiar TV shows, video games, and movies, has nearly 2 billion views and 9 million subscribers. For Andrew, discovering his passions and committing to exploring those in tangible, practical ways was essential for his own mental and physical health, and his daily motivation.[1] Not only that, he's now bringing joy to others through his own passions!

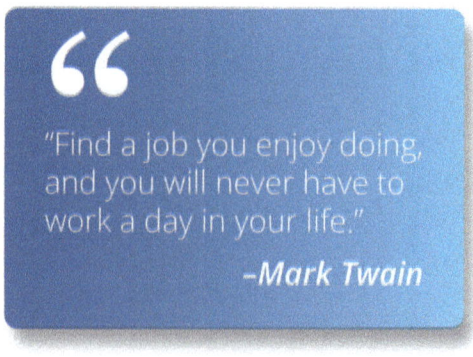

"Find a job you enjoy doing, and you will never have to work a day in your life."
–Mark Twain

For some of us, naming our passions is easy. As soon as we have a chance, we are mentoring others, trying a new recipe, encouraging others, teaching a new course, or getting on the water. For others, being asked about our passions can leave us stumped.

Passions are what inspire and move us. They bring life to our life, and energy to our days. They may be found in our work or our free time, or a combination of those.

What are you passionate about? Write down the activities or interests that most energize you:

_____
_____
_____
_____

Did this come easy or was it difficult? How many passions were you able to name? Being able to identify our passions, and incorporate those into our regular routine, is a great way to:
- improve our physical and emotional health,
- stir our inspiration,
- rejuvenate our relationships, and
- fill us with renewed motivation

---

5   "Why Following Your Passions is Good For You (and How to Get Started)," by Lizz Schumer, The New York Times, October 10, 2018, https://www.nytimes.com/2018/10/10/smarter-living/follow-your-passion-hobbies-jobs-self-care.html

DYNAMIC > STATIC PASSIONS

One common misconception about passions is that they're static. Research shows that they change as we grow and are often developed over time. Jon Jachimowicz is Assistant Professor of Business Administration in the Organizational Behavior Unit at Harvard Business School. He writes this for the *Harvard Business Review*: "believing that passion is fixed can make people less likely to explore new topics—potential new sources of passion." [1]

> "Participants who engaged in hobbies were 34 percent less stressed and 18 percent less sad during the activities, as well as for some time after.
>
> "Real-Time Associations Between Engaging in Leisure and Daily Health and Well-Being," *The Annals of Behavioral Medicine*

If you're having trouble identifying your passion, it's a good sign that this is an opportunity for growth in your life. Spend some time thinking about areas of interest that you have been wanting to explore. Here are some common passions:

What are three passions that you would like to explore in the next month? Write those down.

Rock Climbing	Biking	Teaching	Gardening
Painting	Notes of Encouragement	Ultimate Frisbee	Quilting
Playing Guitar	Organization	Record-Collecting	Astronomy
Golf	Writing Poetry	Animals	Candle Making
Dancing	Kayaking	Yoga	Interior Design
Fishing	Hiking	Sculpting	Swimming
Mentoring	Serving	Hospitality	Travel
Photography	Calligraphy	Gardening	Tennis

Passion 1: _____

Passion 2: _____

Passion 3: _____

---

6   "3 Reasons It's So Hard to 'Follow Your Passions,'" by Jon M. Jachimowicz, Harvard Business Review, October 15, 2019, https://hbr.org/2019/10/3-reasons-its-so-hard-to-follow-your-passion

TWO WORDS OF WARNING:

First, we sometimes reduce our passions to either 1) our work, or 2) our hobbies. The truth is, our passions are bigger than either and transcend them.

Second, research shows that passions are not always what we find the most fun. Sometimes they are deeply challenging, but still bring us energy and motivation. Don't give up on a new potential passion as soon as it gets difficult. Give it enough time to see if it's something that can motivate you.

"You have to be burning with an idea, or a problem, or a wrong that you want to right. If you're not passionate enough from the start, you'll never stick it out."

-Steve Jobs

COMMIT TO EXPLORING NEW PASSIONS

Write down how you will set aside time to explore each new potential passion in the next month. Be as specific as you can. What day of the week will you set aside for this? What time of the day? Give yourself at least *one hour* each week for each passion.

Passion 1:

_____
_____
_____

Passion 2:

_____
_____
_____

Passion 3:

_____
_____
_____

Ch. 3 Motivate Self

⦿ Applied EI: After a month, check back in. How'd you do? Were you able to commit to trying these three new passions out each week? If not, what got in the way? Write it down:

_____

_____

If you were able to stick with your plan, did you enjoy them? Did you find a new passion that you want to include in your regular routine moving forward? If so, write it down now:

_____

If none of these are likely to "stick" for you, return to the above list and select three new passions to explore in the next month. Keep going until you feel like you've established something that is energizing and motivating to you.

The only way we get to new passions is by trial and error. But discovering your personal passions and committing to including those in your daily and weekly schedule will give you energy and motivation when you need it most.
Here's to exploring and developing your passions!

ROUTINE & NOVELTY: EVERY FEW DO SOMETHING NEW

2020 tested our routines—but also demonstrated their power. For some of us, they made the difference during the COVID-19 pandemic between staying motivated and going crazy. Getting up at the same time each day, keeping a regular exercise routine, scheduling Zoom meetings with friends, keeping defined work hours, and getting dressed in our work clothes (even if working offsite) made all the difference. As the COVID-19 pandemic affected all of us, we learned that creating structure in our day helps maintain our mental, social, and physical well-being. Whether we're in a global pandemic or not, routines help us stay healthy and motivated.

Ch. 3 Motivate Self

PERSONALITY SELF-ASSESSMENT: ROUTINE OR NOVELTY

Are you a creature of habit, or are you more inclined to spontaneity? On a scale of 1 to 10, where 1 is the most routine-oriented and 10 is the most spontaneous, how would you describe yourself? Circle your answer:

Routine-Oriented　　　　　　　　　　　　　　　　　　　Spontaneity

1　　2　　3　　4　　5　　6　　7　　8　　9　　10

For those of us who are closer to the routine-oriented end of the spectrum, a regular structure and plan helps provide a sense of security and peace. For those of us on the other end, routines may feel like they suck the excitement out of life. But wherever you are, routines can help improve your motivation.

> "You'll never change your life until you change something you do daily. The secret to your success is found in your daily routine."
>
> –John C. Maxwell

INTRODUCING NEW ROUTINES

Wherever you find yourself on the above self-assessment, let's talk about ways to introduce new routines into your life to improve your motivation: across your Personal, Social, and Work life.

Personal Routines

What areas of your personal life could use more motivation? Maybe it's your physical health and getting more exercise? Or, maybe it's taking time to read more. Or, it could be improving your sleep schedule.

Identify three aspects of your personal life where you feel you could use some help when it comes to a routine:

1. _____

2. _____

3. _____

42

Now, let's get specific in each area about the routine you want to introduce.

Starting with your first area, what sort of a routine would help you create a regular rhythm? For example, if it's getting more exercise, let's say it's committing to 15 minutes of exercise, three days a week. If it's sleep, let's say it's committing to eight hours each night, setting your bedtime and what time you will wake up. Be as specific as possible!

Routine 1._____

Routine 2._____

Routine 3._____

Social Routines

Think about your relationships with family and friends. Where could they benefit from more structure? Maybe it's committing to check in with your parents, or your children, every day. Maybe it's finally agreeing to join that monthly book group you've been putting off. Or, maybe it's committing to an every-other-week dinner with your neighbors as a way of getting to know them better.

Identify three aspects of your social life where you feel you could use some help when it comes to a routine:

1._____

2._____

3._____

Once again, write how you plan to introduce that routine in each area, being as specific as possible:

Routine 1._____

Routine 2._____

Routine 3._____

Work Routines

Lastly, think about how routines could benefit your work. For some of us, we need to make sure we're not working too much by creating and sticking to a work schedule. For others, we could use a set time to start our workday each morning. It could be creating a weekly schedule to post on LinkedIn, encouraging more professional connections and new work opportunities. Or, it may be setting aside a daily lunch hour and taking a walk.

Whatever it might be for you, name three aspects of your work life where you could improve your motivation with a set routine:

1. _____

2. _____

3. _____

Now, be specific, and write a plan for how you will introduce that routine in each area:

Routine 1._____

Routine 2._____

Routine 3._____

At the end of each week, check off each routine that you've completed. This little way of rewarding yourself will encourage you and give you a sense of accomplishment.

> **Applied EI:** Set yourself a reminder to check in on your new routines in 30 days (my phone works best for me). How're they going? Were some a little too ambitious? Or, have you found yourself outgrowing other routines? Most importantly, are they helping?

Take the time to walk through each of your new routines in your Personal, Social, and Work categories, and recalibrate them based on your experience over the past month. Your new routines should be regularly evaluated and re-evaluated to make sure they're giving you both structure and a little push. If they're working as they should, you should notice a boost in your motivation!

Novelty: Every Few, Do Something New

What's the last new activity you tried? Was it a new sport? Visiting a new place? Cooking a new recipe? We all crave novelty—some more than others. Trying something new helps us move forward. It helps us grow. When life feels stagnant, exploring a new activity can be just the thing we need.

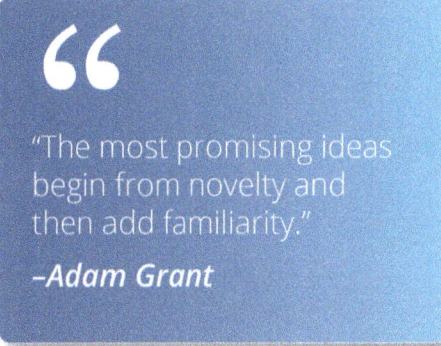

"The most promising ideas begin from novelty and then add familiarity."
–Adam Grant

In addition to inspiring and motivating us, trying new activities is also good for our health. As noted in *Psychology Today,* "The sedentary life contributes to a host of maladies—cardiovascular disease, diabetes, osteoporosis, stroke, hypertension, depression, obesity—that together account for up to 75% of the deaths in industrialized countries."[1]

I love trying new things! In fact, you've probably heard a favorite phrase of mine by now: "For every few, do something new." For every few routine activities, I introduce a new activity to give myself a spark of motivation. It makes a huge difference!

What's a new activity that you've been wanting to try but you've been struggling to start?

Great! Now, what are the obstacles that have been getting in the way? Is it time? Finances? Or something else? Whatever it is, go ahead and name that challenge or challenges:

_____
_____
_____
_____
_____
_____
_____
_____

---

7   "Novelty-Seeking: One of the Keys to Thriving in Life," Psychology Today blog, by Gregg Levoy, April 19, 2018, https://www.psychologytoday.com/us/blog/passion/201804/novelty-seeking-one-the-keys-thriving-in-life

When it comes to this particular challenge, what are some ways that you might be able to help overcome them? If it's finances, could you begin saving a little bit each paycheck until you have enough money? If it's time, what about setting aside time each week to give yourself the pleasure of this new activity. Spend a few minutes right now thinking about how you can overcome these challenges that have previously prevented you from this new activity:

_____
_____
_____
_____

After engaging in your new activity, reflect on how it went. Was it as rewarding as you imagined? More difficult than you expected? Do you think you will do it again, or turn to another new activity? Capture your experience here:

_____
_____
_____
_____
_____
_____
_____

💭 **Applied EI:** Now that you've identified a new activity that you've been wanting to try, named what was stopping you. Create a plan to overcome that challenge and try it out. Why not start over with a new activity? What would you like to try next? Go ahead, write it down:

_____
_____

Return to this exercise as often as you need in order to introduce new activities into your regular routines. As you do, you are sure to notice a boost in your mental health, your overall life satisfaction, and your motivation.

Now that you've set yourself some new routines, and created a plan to introduce new activities, you're well on your way to a balanced life rhythm.

Whether we're working on a long project and struggling to find motivation or we're in a rut and every day feels the same. Having a rhythm of routine and new experiences can help us get in a productive groove. A healthy rhythm that balances routine and novelty will encourage you to stay motivated and improve your work and wellbeing.

MOTIVATING RELATIONSHIPS: COMPETITION, ACCOUNTABILITY, AND ENCOURAGEMENT

We're not meant to go it alone. When it comes to motivation, relationships are essential for keeping us going.

Another important factor in our motivation is relationships. Even if most of our work is done on our own, our interactions with others will motivate us. This happens primarily in three ways: relationships of competition, accountability, and encouragement.

Refer to Pages 60-64 to remind yourself what each of these relationships means, and to find some helpful examples. In their own way, each of these relationships have offered an important source of motivation and helped me to accomplish more than I could on my own. They help me to stay true to my own goals and sense of self, especially when challenges arise.

How about you? What are the relationships of Competition, Accountability, and Encouragement in your life? Let's take some time to identify several examples for each of these categories.

Competition—friends whose successes push you to become more successful:

_____

_____

Accountability—friends who hold you to higher standards:

_____

_____

Encouragement—friends who stand by you regardless of your success:

_____

_____

How do you feel about your lists? Were you able to name three relationships for each category? If not, this provides a clear visual on where you can grow and improve, relationally.

Prioritize to Maximize Impact

Now that you've identified three relationships for each category, think about how important each group has been as a source of motivation in your life. We are all motivated differently. For me, I thrive in competition. But others may do better when they are receiving regular encouragement. And, this order of importance may also change with circumstances. If we're going through an especially difficult time, we may find that relationships of Encouragement become more important.

Generally speaking, how would you rate these three different types of motivating relationships in order of importance (Competition, Accountability, and Encouragement)?

1. _____

2. _____

3. _____

Great! Now that you know which types of relationships are most motivating to you, and have examples of each, take the time to check in with these people when you find yourself struggling with motivation. Pay special attention to the types of relationships that maximize impact in your life. If you need to, think of other relationships that you might want to develop in this high-priority area. Maybe they're relationships that were once close but have since faded away.

> 🧠 **Applied EI:** Is there anything getting in the way of connecting with your relationships of Competition, Accountability, or Encouragement? A job change can mean a relationship of Competition that previously drove you is no longer in your life. Or sometimes, life's busyness causes our regular relationships of Accountability to fizzle and dry out. Or an unexpected move can mean that we no longer speak with someone who was previously essential for our encouragement.
>
> If you're struggling in any of these three areas, take the time to ask yourself why, and then write down the relationship and the reason here:
>
> **Relationship:** _____
>
> **Reason:** _____
> _____
>
> Sometimes something as simple as checking in can revitalize a relationship that has gone quiet. Taking the time to identify any struggling relationships and then doing something about it can open up an entirely new channel of motivation in your life—and likely their life, too!

Emotionally Intelligent individuals know the relationships they can call on when needed and take the initiative to do so, rather than waiting to be contacted. With this plan in place, you're well on your way to improving your EI!

PART II:

THEM

Chapter 4:
IDENTIFY

Have you ever been driving along the highway and just knew what a car was about to do, like change lanes without signaling? It's hard to explain, but after driving for so many years, you've developed the ability to read traffic. You may not always be right, but you're right more often than not.

I've been comparing EI to going on a road trip with friends. Once you've got a good handle on your own "car," you have to get on the road and interact with "them"—the other people that may or may not have a good handle on their own cars.

Those who make strong connections know how to read others. . Whether it's staring out at a crowd of faces from a stage or sitting with one person over a cup of coffee, creating meaningful connections requires being able to pick up on not only what's spoken, but what's unspoken. Being able to read others is a consistent and key mark of Emotional Intelligence.

Research suggests that as much as 90 percent of communication is nonverbal. Rather than putting their emotions into words, people often express how they feel with facial expressions, tone of voice, hand gestures, body movements, and more. Emotions are not as private as we might think. We are routinely putting them on display, and we can read them in others, if we know what to look for.

Reading others' non-verbal communication involves several different components: facial expressions, physical posture, and even tone of voice. Let's spend some time digging into each of these three aspects of non-verbal communication now.

READING FACIAL EXPRESSIONS

How well can you read faces? On a scale of 1 to 10, how would you describe yourself? Circle your answer:

Least Skilled   Most Skilled

1   2   3   4   5   6   7   8   9   10

Personal Assessment

Take this online quiz from Greater Good Magazine to measure how well you can read others' emotions by their facial expressions: https://greatergood.berkeley.edu/quizzes/ei_quiz/take_quiz.

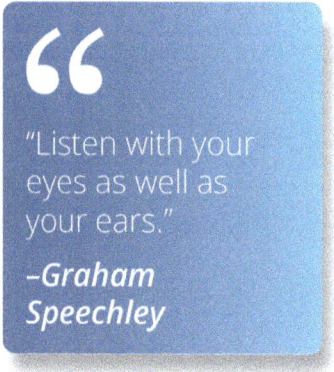

"Listen with your eyes as well as your ears."

–Graham Speechley

Ch. 4: Identify

How'd you do? What was your score out of 20? How did your self-assessment compare to your quiz results, better or worse?

_____
_____
_____
_____

Which emotions did you struggle to identify? Contempt, perhaps? Or pride? Were there any emotions that you confused with another emotion?

_____
_____
_____
_____
_____
_____
_____

From the tilt of the head to the curve of the lips, facial expressions are complex! You might have been surprised by the level of detail involved in recognizing emotions. You may also have learned some new terms, such as the Duchenne Smile. What are one or two things that you learned about reading emotions from this quiz?

_____
_____
_____
_____

As you now know, interpreting facial expressions isn't something you're either born with or not. It's a skill that can be developed with time, intentional effort, and practice. Improving this ability is a great way to improve your EI.

💡 **Applied EI:** Spend some time this week really paying attention to others' faces while you're speaking. What emotions do you recognize? Write them down after each interaction, noting how they fit with what was being verbally communicated (or not!).

After a week of practice, return to this quiz and take it again. How'd you do the second time? Did you improve? Mark your score here, identifying any emotions you'd still like to improve:

_____
_____
_____
_____
_____
_____
_____
_____

READING PHYSICAL POSTURE

How aware are you of your physical posture? Some of us were raised to "always stand up straight." Others don't give it a fleeting thought. But how we hold our physical posture can communicate loads of information to others—oftentimes, without us even realizing it. Crossing your arms can tell someone you're disagreeing with them or are closed off to the conversation, for example. While sitting up straight and leaning slightly forward can convey interest and attention.

Being aware of these differences is helpful to make sure you're communicating what you intend to. It's also essential for reading non-verbal cues and connecting with others. Generally speaking, there are two different physical postures in interpersonal communication: Open and Closed.[1]

Someone with an **Open Posture** keeps their body, you guessed it, open and exposed to others. They keep their arms open, making themselves vulnerable, which communicates a sense of trust and a willingness to engage. Open Postures are interpreted as friendly and confident.

Someone with a **Closed Posture**, in contrast, has blocked or hidden their body in some way. This may involve crossing their arms or hunching over. Closed Postures can communicate anxiety, fear, disapproval, and a lack of interest.

Now that you're familiar with these different postures and what they mean, pay special attention to other people in conversation and take note of when you notice each type.

When did you notice someone this week with a **Closed Posture**? What did that communicate to you?

_____

_____

_____

_____

When did you notice someone this week with an Open Posture? What did that communicate to you?

_____

_____

---

8   "Understanding Body Language and Facial Expressions," Kendra Cherry, September 28, 2019, https://www.verywellmind.com/understand-body-language-and-facial-expressions-4147228

Ch. 4: Identify

_____

_____

As you're engaging others in conversation, continue to pay attention to their physical posture. Is it Open or Closed? What does this tell you about their level of engagement? Is there anything that you need to do differently to create better engagement?

"93/7 Rule: 93% of communication occurs through nonverbal behavior & tone; only 7% of communication takes place through the use of words."

–John Stoker

TONE OF VOICE

"Don't use that tone of voice with me!" You've heard that one before, right? Probably from a parent or another person of authority. It highlights the importance of tone of voice for communication. It's not only what we say that matters, *but* how we say it. With our tone of voice, we can communicate excitement or disappointment, confidence or anxiety, sadness or anger—beyond our words. Even the phrase, "I'm sorry," can come across as sincere or sarcastic, depending on the tone of voice.

Like facial expressions and physical posture, tone of voice falls under non-verbal communication. Paying attention to other people's tone of voice is a critical way to connect. In fact, research shows that closing our eyes can actually improve our ability to understand.[1] Sometimes, this is because we need to focus, but other times, it's because some people are better skilled at hiding their emotions facially than in their voice.

"Listening matters. Actually considering what people are saying and the ways in which they say it can, I believe, lead to improved understanding of others at work or in your personal relationships."

–Dr. Michael Kraus, Psychologist at Yale University

When was a time that your tone of voice communicated something you didn't intend?

_____

_____

_____

_____

When was a time you picked up on something in someone else's tone that didn't come through in their words? What did you notice? Did you bring it up? If so, how did that go?

_____

_____

_____

_____

Listening carefully to others' tone of voice as a way of picking up on what they're really saying, beyond their words, and being intentional about your own tone, is essential for creating meaningful connections.

LISTEN CURIOUSLY

Speaking of listening, how good are you at it? Would others describe you as a good listener, always present and attentive, or as someone who's easily distracted?

Let's find out.

Listening Assessment

On a scale of 1 to 10, where 1 is the least skilled at listening and 10 is the most skilled, how would you describe yourself? Circle your answer:

    Poor Listener   Excellent Listener

    1   2   3   4   5   6   7   8   9   10

Now, let's ask someone else for their take on your skills. Ask a trusted friend or family member how well they think you listen to others. On the same scale, how did they describe you? Circle their answer:

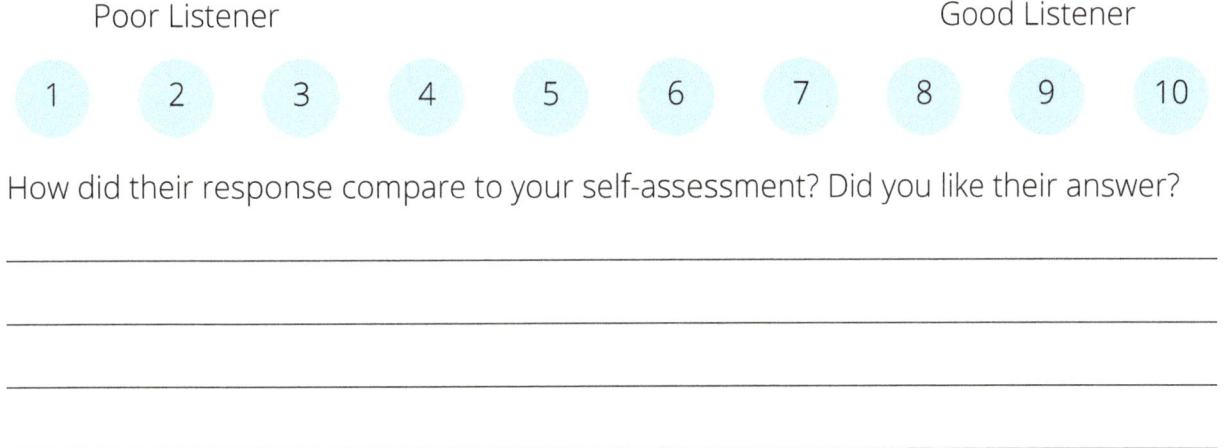

Poor Listener   Good Listener

1   2   3   4   5   6   7   8   9   10

How did their response compare to your self-assessment? Did you like their answer?

_____

_____

_____

_____

 "The biggest communication problem is we do not listen to understand. We listen to reply."

—Stephen R. Covey, *The 7 Habits of Highly Effective People*

Improving Your Listening

For many of us, actively listening to others, with curiosity and without distraction, can be a real challenge. Here are a few suggestions to improve your ability to listen with curiosity:

- Avoid judgements
- Maintain eye contact
- Don't interrupt (that includes finishing other people's sentences!)
- Provide non-verbal cues that show you're listening (head nod or mirroring)
- Ask clarifying questions
- Avoid distracting humor
- Stop shifting the conversation to your own experience
- After they finish speaking, take a breath before responding.
- *Don't Plan Your Response*

One of the primary distractions is focusing on how we will respond. We all do this! When you notice this happening, allow your thoughts to return to what the other person is saying—without judgment. Ask for clarification if you missed anything. If absolutely necessary, apologize and jot yourself a one or two word reminder of something you need to respond to. Otherwise, when the other person is speaking, simply allow yourself to take in what's being shared—verbally and non-verbally.

Misalignment in Verbal & Non-Verbal Communication

When we're really attending to what the other person is saying, and how they're saying it, we may very well notice a misalignment in verbal and non-verbal speech. Noticing this difference requires attentive listening, but it can help you connect on an even deeper level than merely listening to what's being said

As you listen to others with curiosity, notice whether their face, posture, and hand gestures match their words. If their message is that they have some exciting news to share, is that mirrored in their expression? Likewise, if it's painful news, do they look saddened? A misalignment in verbal and nonverbal messages can reveal that something deeper is going on. Picking up on this misalignment can help you identify more than what's simply being spoken. It can help you connect and ultimately address the real issue.

Can you remember a time when you picked up on a difference between someone's verbal and non-verbal communication? If so, reflect on how you noticed it. Was it their physical posture? Their facial expression? Their tone of voice? What do you think it meant?

_____
_____
_____
_____
_____
_____

Steps to Improve

Returning to the above Listening Assessment, think about the score you gave yourself and the score you received. No matter how skilled we might be in this area, we all have room for improvement.

What challenges are getting in the way of your ability to listen with curiosity? Are they distractions? Defensiveness? Something else? Capture those challenges here.

___

What steps can you take right now to improve on listening with curiosity?

___

Listening with curiosity, as to better understand what others are communicating, helps you improve your EI and create meaningful connections.

> 💡 **Applied EI:** This next week, really focus on listening with curiosity, and see if you notice any misalignments in verbal and non-verbal communication. As you notice those, you may bring them up in conversation and ask if anything else is going on that they would like to talk about. Capture that experience here

___

REVERSING OTHERS' FEELINGS

A doctor's job starts with, but doesn't end with, listening curiously. She must then use what she's heard to help her patient get better. Likewise, caring about and for other people frequently means helping reverse—i.e. deal with and overcome—negative feelings. In the words of U2's classic song, "One," we *get* to carry each other.

Beyond identifying others' feelings, another important part of EI is the ability to 'reverse' a person's feelings. Obviously, negative feelings are the ones that need to be changed. That can be very difficult.

When was a time that someone helped reverse negative feelings in your life? What did they do that was helpful? Likewise, what did they not do that was helpful?

_____
_____
_____
_____
_____
_____
_____

When it comes to your own interactions with others, can you remember a time when you were able to identify a negative emotion in someone else and were able to help that person with that? What did you do that was helpful?

_____
_____
_____
_____
_____
_____
_____

Ask Before Offering Help

Those who live with a high EI know when to actively help and when to simply listen. How? By asking, "Are you looking for help or just a listening ear?" By taking the time to check in, you'll avoid offering a solution they're not looking for.

> 💡 **Applied EI:** In this chapter, we covered several ways to identify what others are feeling. Which area are you feeling most comfortable and confident in?
>
> _____
>
> In which of these areas do you want to improve? What are some steps you can take in the next month? Capture those now.
>
> _____
> _____
> _____
> _____

Chapter 5:
EMPATHIZE

From Connect Through Emotional Intelligence, page 82

It's one thing to understand the other "cars" on the road—to read what they are doing and respond accordingly. It is another to see those cars as people. You've probably heard the expression "The Good Samaritan." It comes from a story Jesus told his followers. In that parable, the respected religious leaders ignored a badly wounded person and treated him as an inconvenience. It was only the Samaritan who saw him as a person. That is the challenge of this chapter—learning to see others as people with thoughts, feelings, and needs that are just as important as our own.

If our work on Emotional Intelligence has an hourglass shape, empathy is at the center.

Everything we've talked about up to this point leads to empathy. And everything we will talk about from this point forward will come back to it.

As should be clear after reading Chapter 5 of Connect through Emotional Intelligence, empathy involves allowing ourselves to move beyond identifying what others are feeling to actually feeling it.

From Connect Through Emotional Intelligence, page 84

If we're going to connect with others, we must move beyond just identifying what they are feeling. We must truly understand their perspective. We must empathize with them. Empathy is the center and central point of EI.

Empathy is critical for personal and professional connections. And, due to a number of factors, our need to work on empathy is more important than ever. One long-term study indicates that the average American is less empathic today than 75 percent of Americans 30 years ago. [1]

---

10 https://brandgenetics.com/empathy-statistics-for-business

Ch 5: Empathize

At the same time, our interest in empathy is on the rise. The number of papers in psychology journals on the topic of empathy has increased dramatically in recent years, and Google search results for "empathy" have skyrocketed since the early 2000s.[1] Never before have we been more interested in empathy, and never before have we been worse at it.

> In a meta-analysis of US citizen empathy test scores conducted over the past 30 years, today's average American is less empathic than 75 percent of Americans 30 years ago.

Google Search Interest in "Empathy"

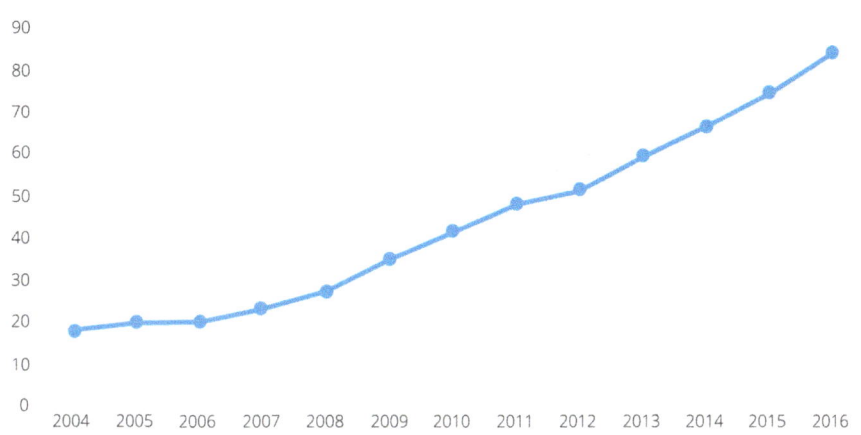

Source: Google Trends

While women are generally more empathetic than men, empathy is something that all of us can grow in. There are several ways to help build this skill, but let's begin by spending some time reflecting on where you have experienced empathy.

Models of Empathy

Who is a model of empathy in your life?

_____

When was a time you experienced their empathy personally? Be as specific as possible. Was it their language? Their expression? Something else?

_____

_____

---

11 https://greatergood.berkeley.edu/article/item/whats_the_matter_with_empathy

Ch 5: Empathize

_____
_____
_____
_____
_____

Noticing these aspects of empathy from your interactions is a helpful way to improve your empathy. Moving beyond that interaction, what are some traits of other empathetic people in your life? How have those traits impacted your own life?

_____
_____
_____
_____
_____
_____
_____
_____

> "When we honestly ask ourselves which person in our lives mean the most to us, we often find that it is those who, instead of giving advice, solutions, or cures, have chosen rather to share our pain and touch our wounds with a warm and tender hand."
> –Henri Nouwen

Challenges to Empathy

Let's take a minute to think about some of the challenges to empathy. We live in a time when empathy can be hard to come by. Political, religious, and socio-economical differences tend to divide us, making it more difficult to empathize with those around us.

In your own experience, what challenges have gotten in the way of your ability to empathize with others? Was it stress? Political, religious, or other divisions? Something else?

_____
_____
_____
_____
_____
_____
_____
_____

What are some steps you can take to help address these challenges?

_____
_____
_____
_____
_____
_____
_____
_____

Empathy Quiz

There are a number of tools to measure your ability to empathize with others. One quick and free method is the Greater Good Empathy Quiz, which draws on the work of a number of different researchers in this area. You can take this brief assessment here:

https://greatergood.berkeley.edu/quizzes/take_quiz/empathy

How'd you do? How do you feel about your score?

_____

Did you rate higher on "affective empathy" (*feeling* what others feel) or "cognitive empathy" (*understanding* others' perspectives and feelings)?

_____

In what ways would you like to improve your empathy?

_____
_____
_____

No matter your score, remember that empathy is not a fixed trait but a learned skill and behavior. We can all improve if we're willing to put in the work. So let's get to work by looking at some ways you can improve your ability to empathize with others.

EXPLORE THEIR PERSPECTIVE

Who's your favorite literary character? Or, who's your favorite character from a TV show or movie?

_____

Now, when you think of that character, where do you picture them? What are they doing?

_____
_____
_____

Good. Now that you have a clear picture, how would you describe what they're feeling? And, more importantly, why are they feeling that way?

_____
_____

Ch 5: Empathize

_____
_____
_____
_____
_____

Reading books and watching the right kind of movies is a great way to explore other people's perspectives. And, when we're intentionally exploring not just what they're feeling, but why, we're actively building our empathy muscles.

WALKING IN SOMEONE ELSE'S SHOES

"At our best, we practice empathy, imagining ourselves in the lives and circumstances of others." President George W. Bush offered this call for empathy at a 2016 memorial service for fallen police officers. Sometimes, we need to *imagine* ourselves into empathy. This is especially true when our experiences are very different from others. When we cannot actually feel what others feel.

> "You think your pain and your heartbreak are unprecedented in the history of the world, but then you read. It was books that taught me that the things that tormented me most were the very things that connected me with all the people who were alive, who had ever been alive."
>
> –James Baldwin

From Connect Through Emotional Intelligence, page 91

One of the biggest mistakes we can make when connecting with others is judging how others speak or act based on our own experience, rather than trying to understand and feel theirs. Correcting this mistake can go a long way in helping us to create meaningful connections, especially with those whose perspective is different from our own.

To improve our empathy, we must actively avoid judging other people's actions, decisions, or speech based on our own experience. To do that, we need to step outside of our own experience and allow ourselves to feel what it's like to walk in their shoes.

> "Self-absorption in all its forms kills empathy, let alone compassion. When we focus on ourselves, our world contracts as our problems and preoccupations loom large. But when we focus on others, our world expands. Our own problems drift to the periphery of the mind and so seem smaller, and we increase our capacity for connection-or compassionate action."
>
> –Daniel Goleman

An Exercise in Empathy

Think of someone you know, maybe a family member or a friend, who has had a difficult experience recently. Write down their name:

_____

How would you describe their mood lately? Are they sad? Disappointed? Perhaps they're frustrated. Try to be as specific as you can in describing their emotions.

_____
_____
_____

Good—now you're noticing how someone else is feeling. This is the first step toward empathy. Now think about what's been going on in their life that has caused their feelings. Again, get specific here.

_____
_____
_____

If you were to have the same experience, how would you feel? Similar? Different? Really try to put yourself in their shoes, and describe what you are feeling:

_____
_____
_____

Great job putting yourself in someone else's experience, and allowing yourself to really feel what they are experiencing! Now that you've taken the time to do that, how might you respond to this family member or friend? What might be some helpful ways for you to engage, based on what you have allowed yourself to feel from their experience?

_____
_____
_____
_____
_____
_____
_____
_____
_____
_____

> "You never really understand a person until you consider things from his point of view...until you climb into his skin and walk around in it."
> –Harper Lee, To Kill A Mockingbird

Applied EI: Now that you've allowed yourself to feel what someone you know is feeling, take it a step further this week. When you're listening to or watching the news and you hear about someone you deeply disagree with, take a few minutes to put yourself in your shoes.

Based on what you know of their experience, how would you describe how they must be feeling? Can you put yourself in that experience yourself? Can you imagine acting or responding in a similar way?

Each time we allow ourselves to feel what others are feeling—especially those whose experience is different from our own—we are expanding our empathy. Take this approach anytime you hear of someone acting in a way that you don't understand. It will help you grow your Emotional Intelligence and create deeper connections with others.

Chapter 6:
EXPLORE

From Connect Through Emotional Intelligence, page 96

We've all been there. Traffic is crawling along, and your exit is coming up. You turn on your blinker and hope for the best. The car to your right shows mercy and lets you merge. You slide in and give them a quick "thank you" wave. Without a word, you have connected with them.

Approaching new conversations can feel like a game of exploration.

Personally, I look at every interaction as an opportunity for discovery. The same can be true for you, if you know how to approach them.

From Connect Through Emotional Intelligence, page 96

There's more to EI than identifying what others are feeling and empathizing with them. You need to engage with them, to connect on some level. Some time ago, I discovered the ALAER process to help me effectively engage with others, using the steps: Ask, Listen, Acknowledge, Explore, and Respond.

I like to refer to this process as flying a kite. Like flying a kite, it involves repeatedly checking in and renegotiating. If you simply let out a little string and hope to fly, you're going to be disappointed. Things are soon going to come to an abrupt end—as my son has found out! Similarly, if you're looking to connect with others and you simply ask a question and stop, you're going to be sorely disappointed. In both cases, you need to do more to gain traction and keep things going. When you're flying a kite, you need to regularly check the connection with the line and the same is true in connecting with others, using the ALAER approach.

.

Ch. 6 Explore

The ALAER approach is all about giving you another tool for your toolbox, helping you to create meaningful connections with others. In this chapter, I want to help you practice each of these important five steps: Ask, Listen, Acknowledge, Explore, and Respond. Each of these points are like the edges of a kite—they all require constant attention! And the response, when you finally get there, is where you "grab the wind." But it won't work if you haven't engaged in all of the other points.

ASK QUESTIONS

How do you feel about starting conversations with other people? Does it come naturally to you? Or is it a challenge that makes you anxious?

Think of a recent time when you started a conversation. Was it easy or hard to start? Easy or hard to maintain? Easy or hard to end?

_____
_____
_____
_____

Ch. 6 Explore

If you answered "hard" to any of the questions above, what are the ways you'd like to grow in your conversational skills?

_____

_____

_____

_____

Conversation Starters

One of the best ways to initiate meaningful conversation is by asking thoughtful questions. It shows that you're interested in learning more about someone. These questions may differ depending on the situation, but here is a list of helpful suggestions to try out:

- What's your story?//
- Where did you grow up?
- If you weren't here, what would you be doing?
- What's been the best part of your week?
- The next time you have some free time, what would you like to do?
- Which city have you visited that you'd most like to return to?
- Do you have any hobbies you're enjoying lately?
- Reading anything interesting right now?
- What one book would you not want to be without on a long trip?
- Are you working on anything that you're enjoying?
- What's your favorite part of your job?
- Where would you like to be in five years?

Try these out, see how it goes, and notice which ones you're most comfortable with. And, of course, feel free to make them your own, using language that feels most natural to you.

Ch. 6 Explore

Get Creative

Some conversation starters can feel a little too familiar. If you're looking to create a memorable conversation, get creative. One comedian recently shared in an interview that his favorite question to ask when he's in a new environment is, "Have you ever seen a ghost?" Without fail, he says, someone always has an interesting story to share!

What's the best question you've heard for starting a new conversation?

_____
_____
_____

What are some questions you would like to use to create conversation?

_____
_____
_____
_____
_____

The questions we ask set the stage for the interactions we have with others. Having favorite go-to conversation starter questions in your back pocket is a great way to create meaningful and memorable conversations!

LISTEN ACTIVELY

How well do you stay present in a conversation? After asking a question, the next step in the ALAER approach is Listening Actively. Here's a description of Active Listening:

This means not waiting for others to finish so you can respond. Show the other person that you're really hearing what is being said by using your nonverbal cues. While the other person is speaking, make sure that you're maintaining eye contact, showing interest with both your facial expressions and your body posture. Also, ensure that you're not distracted, either by anything else going on nearby or your own thoughts.

Ch. 6 Explore

We can easily find ourselves distracted in a conversation, even if it's one we started! What are some of the common obstacles you face when it comes to listening?

_____
_____
_____
_____
_____

Great! Now pay attention to those and see if you can identify them in the moment and make corrections in your next conversation. Also, take a moment to revisit the active listening skills found in the "Improving Your Listening" section of Chapter 4.

"Active listening is not only a matter of making yourself available to hear someone talk, but it is showing the sender, physically, that you are receiving and understanding their message on all levels."

–Susan C. Young

Scales of Listening

We listen at varying degrees. Sometimes, we're just listening so that we can begin speaking. Other times, we're listening not only to understand what the other person is sharing, but to understand them. These different ways of listening lead to increasing depths of connection.

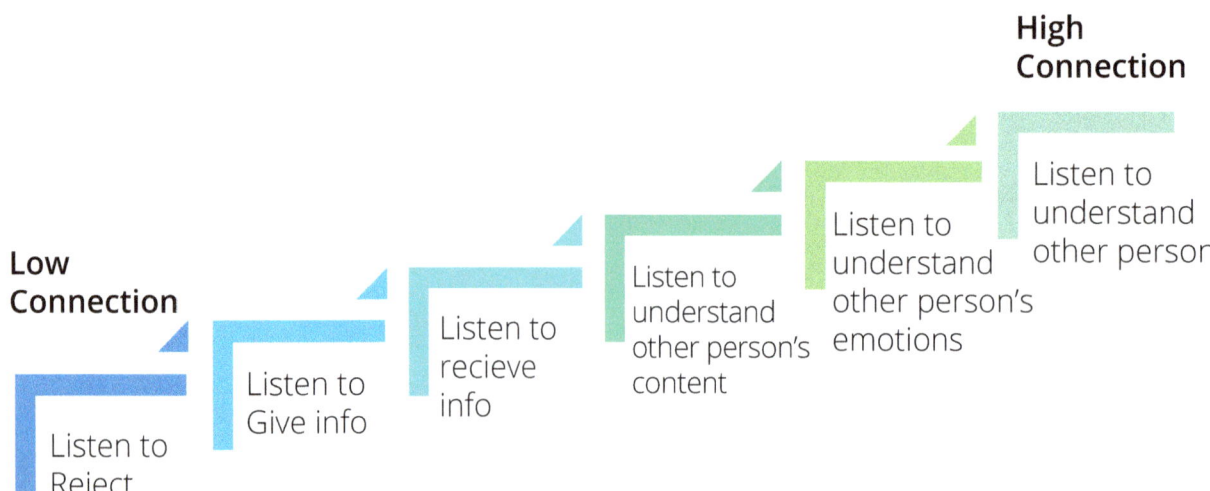

Ch. 6 Explore

With the above scale of listening in mind, can you think of a time when you were at each of these levels? When was a time you moved beyond "Listen to Reject" or "Listen to Give Information" to a higher level?

_____
_____
_____
_____
_____
_____
_____
_____
_____

Continue to identify challenges to actively listening, and make adjustments as needed. Soon, you will notice improvements in your ability to stay focused and listen, which will lead to a better understanding of them as people!

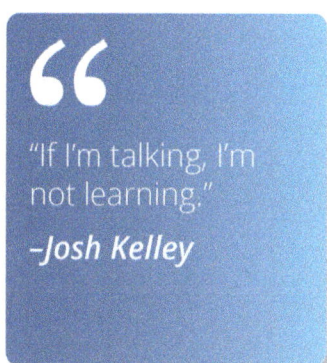

"If I'm talking, I'm not learning."
–Josh Kelley

💡 Applied EI: As you familiarize yourself with these different levels of listening, you will be able to identify where you are in any given conversation, and make steps for improvement. This next week, following a conversation, take note of which level you were at, and ask what you could do differently next time to improve your connection.

ACKNOWLEDGE THE HEART

When the other person finishes speaking, that's your time to show that you've been actively listening. If you immediately move on, they will not feel heard, appreciated, or understood. You're likely to lose them, as soon as you start speaking.

Before saying anything, it's critical to acknowledge the heart of what they just shared. Reflecting what's just been said, in your own words, is an essential way to show others that you've been following what they've shared.

77

From Connect Through Emotional Intelligence, page 98

When the other person has finished speaking, without interrupting them, pause for a second or two to make sure they are really done, then acknowledge what was said with a statement like, "I hear you saying...Did I get that right?" Then, acknowledge how the other person feels. You can say, "That must have made you feel frustrated." Or, "I can imagine you were celebrating after that!" Check to make sure that what you're describing is accurate—look for a nod or some sort of agreement—before continuing.

Next, show that you understand why they feel that way. You can say something like, "If that would have happened to me, I would have felt the same." Or share an example of a similar experience from your own life. But if you do share one of your own experiences, keep it short and intentionally bring it back to what the other person has shared. This will help avoid shifting the focus to yourself.

The only way to acknowledge the heart of what has just been shared is by making sure you're actively listening. Acknowledging the heart includes three parts:

01 INTRO: "I hear you saying...", or "It sounds like..."

02 REFLECTION: Your paraphrase of what has just been said. Use your words, not theirs.

03 CONFIRMATION: "...Is that right?", or "Did I get that straight?"

When the other person has acknowledged that you've understood them, then validate their experience and/or feelings. "Wow, that sounds like a really intense experience!" you might say. Or, "I imagine I'd feel that way, too, if that were me."

Validating their experience and feelings shows that you've not only understood what they experienced, but *why* they feel as they do, and that you can relate. If you bring up a similar experience from your own life to show that you understand, keep it short and bring it back to their experience—don't assume they will see the connection! Keep their experience and their feelings the focus.

Try it Out

Acknowledging the heart is something we don't always do, even when we're actively listening. The next time you're in a conversation, put it into practice. If you're feeling self-conscious, you might find it helpful to ask someone you trust to help you practice:

Ask them, "What was the highlight of your day?" As you actively listen to what they share, practice acknowledging the heart, using the above steps.

Repeat this practice until it comes naturally. You will likely find that other people are happy to practice with you, as they will feel heard, acknowledged, and appreciated!

EXPLORE CURIOUSLY

The first thing people share is rarely all they have to share. For most people, it takes time, trust, and encouragement to open up. That's where you come in! When it comes to listening with the ALAER approach, the key is to help others go deeper than the surface-level sharing. You can guide others by helping them explore more.

> "When a person starts out talking to you about some bothersome problem, you generally hear only the 'presenting problem.' Active Listening effectively facilitates the helpe to move through the presenting problem and finally get down to the core problem."
>
> –Dr. Thomas Gordon

Exploratory Questions

One way to help others get below the surface is to ask exploratory questions. Exploratory Questions build on what's been shared and show, not only that you have been actively listening, but that you're curious to learn more.

Exploratory Questions can be as simple as, "Can you tell me more about why that was important to you?" or, "Can you flesh that out for me?" But be as specific as possible. For example, let's say that you've been listening to someone share the highlight of their day, which was hearing from a family member they hadn't spoken with for a while. You might ask more about this particular family member.

"Do they typically stay in touch, or do you tend to be the one who reaches out?" you could ask.

You've acknowledged the focus of what was shared—connection with a distant family member—while allowing them to share more about why that distance is happening. They may choose to respond to your question by acknowledging who tends to reach out more, but this will also give them space to go deeper into the reason for their distance.

Asking Exploratory Questions helps others get to the heart of what's being shared, without being heavy-handed, forceful, or prying. The goal is to help others explore by being an active and curious learner.

Exploratory Questions Practice

Now it's your turn. To each prompt, write in the Exploratory Question you'd ask to help move each conversation further.

Prompt 1: "I'm doing great, thanks! I've just gotten back from vacation, and it was exactly what I needed!"

Exploratory Question:

_____

_____

_____

Prompt 2: "It's going okay. Not much is new on this end. But I did finally get to check out that book you recommended. You were right. It was helpful."

Exploratory Question:

_____

_____

_____

Prompt 3: "Actually, I'm not doing so well. I got some really difficult news today. These things often come when we're not expecting them, huh?"

Exploratory Question:

_____

_____

_____

_____

As you walked through each of these practice prompts, you likely noticed that they increase in vulnerability and depth. At each step, acknowledging the heart of what is being shared and asking Exploratory Questions requires asking increasingly more intimate questions.

As you ask Exploratory Questions, be careful not to press others further than they're comfortable. Follow their lead.

RESPOND

Before you respond, check in with all of your ALAER points. Remember, it's like flying a kite. Returning to each tip will help prevent the conversation from crashing before it's really taken off.

The temptation for most of us in conversation is to respond immediately to what's been shared with our own perspective. The ALAER approach to connection helps correct this temptation by reserving your response to the very last step. In fact, you may very well take several trips around the Ask–Listen–Acknowledge–Explore sequence *before* you offer a response.

Only after you have done this several times, when you have a full picture of the other person's situation and experience, should you finally respond with your own perspective or offer a suggestion. When you have done this several times before responding, you'll avoid the mistake of assuming you know what they need. Instead, you'll be able to speak into what the other person actually needs.

The point of the ALAER approach is not simply to understand what others are sharing. It is to demonstrate to them that you understand. You'll likely respond in a way that affirms all of the ways you've been actively listening, understanding, and exploring.

Your response may very well include offering your personal wisdom, but it will most certainly be informed by all that you have learned throughout the course of the conversation at-hand.

What was a time when you remember someone responding to something you shared in a helpful way?

_____
_____
_____
_____

What did they *say* that was helpful?

_____
_____
_____
_____

What did they *do* that was helpful?

_____
_____
_____
_____
_____

Variety of Responses

There are several potential responses to every interaction that follows the ALAER approach, increasing in involvement:

01 **Empathy.** In some cases, the most appropriate response is simply to show the other person that you understand what they're going through. This may be because there is no viable solution for their situation. Or maybe what they need most is to be understood. In these cases, the best you can do is to remind them that they're not alone. If your response is empathy, it will probably make sense to set a time to check in with them, and to see if their situation has improved.

02 **Recommendation.** After listening and exploring, you may have a helpful recommendation for them. Be clear and specific. Make sure that they see how your recommendation connects directly to what they've shared. Invite them to ask follow-up questions about your recommendation. Together, all these steps will help them to trust that you're working towards their best interests.

03 **Offer to Help.** Your response may involve getting involved, either by referring them to someone else and offering to make an introduction or by helping them personally. Make sure that 1) this assistant is something they want, and 2) that you'll carry through. Again, be as specific as possible on what it is that you're offering to do, when you plan to do it, and how you will follow up.

When was a time you offered to help someone after listening to him/her share? What help did you offer? Was it received well? If so, what was helpful? If not, what could you do differently next time?

_____
_____
_____
_____
_____
_____
_____
_____
_____
_____
_____

💡 **Applied EI:** The ALAER approach can offer a helpful structure for many of the "connecting through empathy" skills we've explored so far together. Practice this structure and make it your own.

Remember, the point is not simply to understand, but to show that you understand. As long as you're able to do that, it's serving its purpose!

PART III:

US

Chapter 7: BUILDING

You've got your car under control, you're working with the other cars on the highway, but now you've got to work together with all your friends in their own cars so you can get to your destination together. You glance down at your phone to read the text thread (Shame on you—eyes on the road!). One friend just sent a cat gif, another says they need to use the bathroom and wants to get off on the next exit. The "alpha" of the group (is that you?) says they should just hold it. Yeah, everyone is working towards the same objective, but there might be some bumps in the road.

Connecting with others starts with building relationships. That's obvious, but those with a high EI have the skills required to create new and meaningful relationships and actively look for these opportunities.

When it comes to connecting and engaging with others, we are talking about situations that involve social skills. More important to your professional advancement than any technical skills are the social skills that help you navigate social settings with confidence and ease. The good news is that, no matter how anxious you feel in social situations, these skills can be learned, developed, and improved.

In this chapter, I want to explore how to put your EI to work in the area of building new relationships. Let's start with an active reflection on the five levels of friendship in your life.

FIVE LEVELS OF FRIENDSHIP

Your closest friends were once strangers. All friendships start somewhere. Over time and with intentionality, they can grow closer and closer. But, without intentionality, they can drift towards casual friendships or losing touch entirely. When this happens, you can miss out on the deeper friendships that you really desire and are a critical component of life.

Ch. 7 Building

According to the English anthropologist Robin Dunbar, humans tend to have about 150 people involved in their life (social media followers aside!).[1] Of course, some of these relationships are much closer than others, and they get fewer in number as they increase in intimacy. When you get down to the closest people in your life, we're really only talking about three to five people, max.

In *Connect through Emotional Intelligence*, I introduced five levels of friendship: Stranger, Acquaintance, Casual Friend, Close Friend, and Intimate Friend. Each of these levels have a unique role in our lives, and they move from the most broad and numerous to the most intimate and fewest number of people involved:

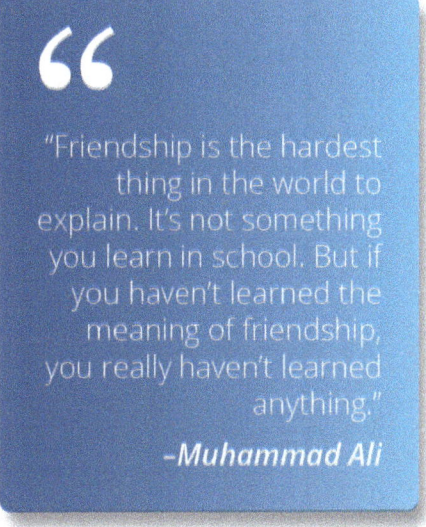

> "Friendship is the hardest thing in the world to explain. It's not something you learn in school. But if you haven't learned the meaning of friendship, you really haven't learned anything."
>
> *–Muhammad Ali*

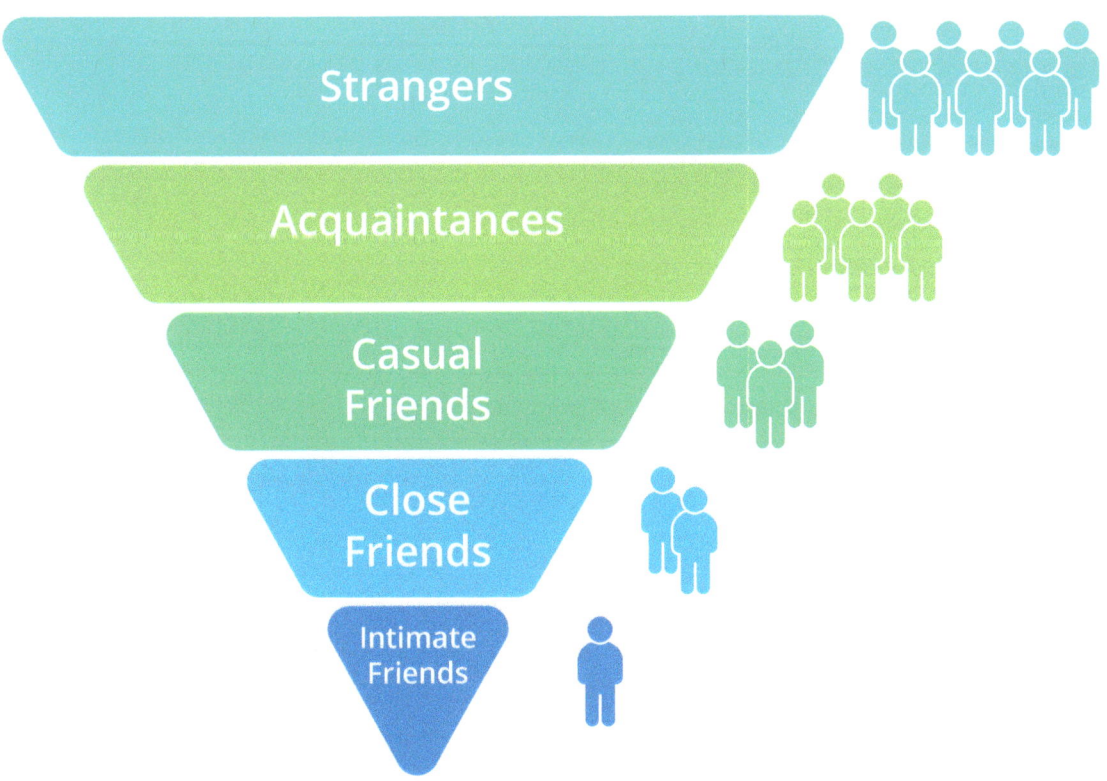

---

12 "How Many Friends Do You Need?" https://psychcentral.com/lib/how-many-friends-do-you-need

Ch. 7 Building

Refer to these descriptions in Connect through Emotional Intelligence if you need to be reminded of the meaning of each type of friendship. With the exception of the first category, Strangers, list people in your life who fit into each category:

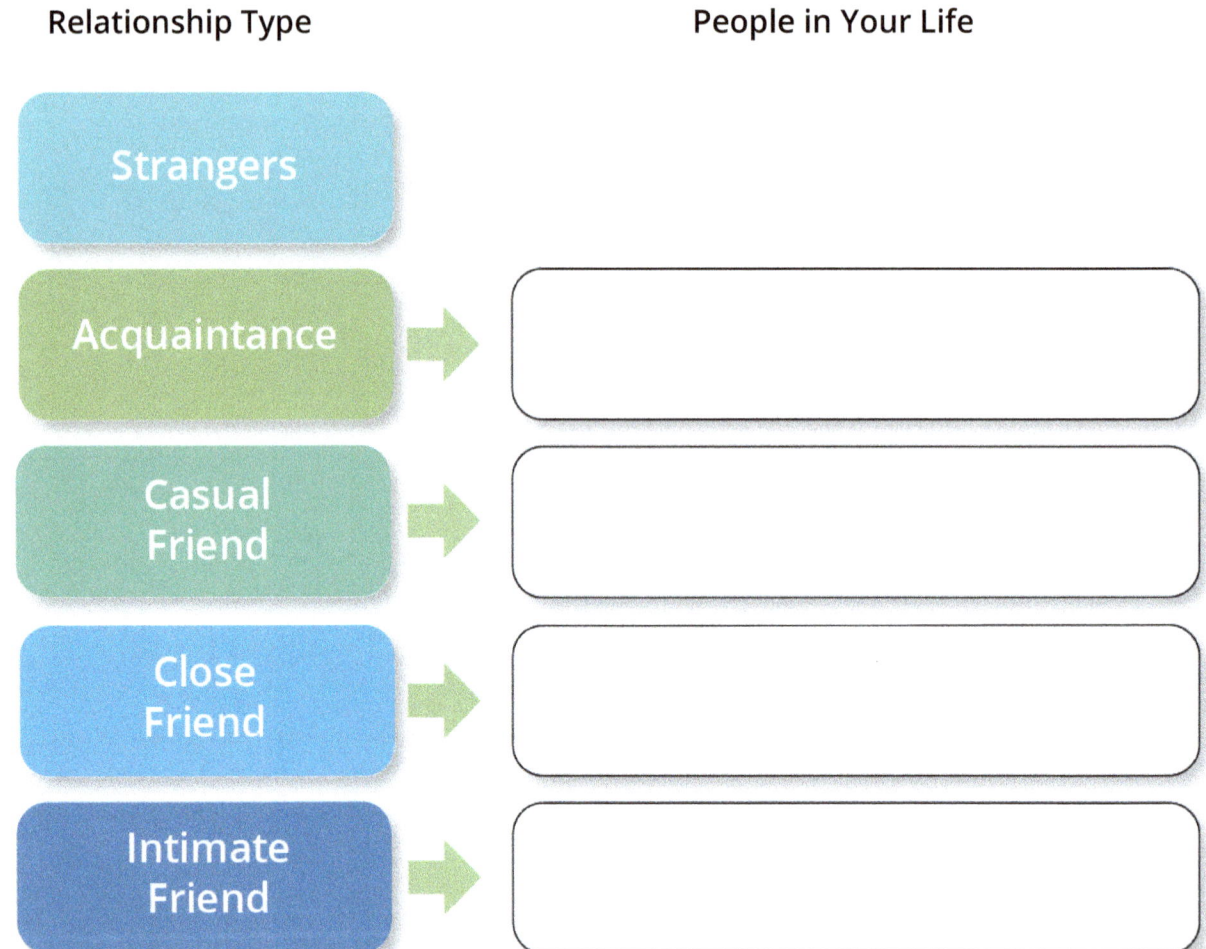

Relationship Type — **People in Your Life**

- Strangers
- Acquaintance
- Casual Friend
- Close Friend
- Intimate Friend

Now, looking over your responses, where do you feel like you're lacking in friendships? In which of these areas do you want to grow?

_____

_____

_____

When we're lacking enough friends at the more intimate levels, we become lonely. This can happen for a number of reasons—such as moving to a new city or being overly busy with work. Whatever the reason, this can be addressed and improved. But it's going to take some intentional work on your part!

Looking at those specific names, are there any friendships on that list that you would like to move to a deeper level of friendship? If so, write those down now, listing their current category and what level of friendship you'd like them to move to.

Name:	Current Category:	Goal Category:

Moving friends to closer levels of intimacy involves intentionality. How that plays out should reflect what you know to be true of yourself and the other person. This intentional effort to get to know someone at a deeper level can be as easy as asking someone to grab a cup of coffee to joining you for an activity that you enjoy, perhaps watching or playing soccer.

Who is someone in your life who has intentionally invested in your friendship? How have they done that in ways that helped you both grow closer? How might they be a model for you?

_____

_____

Ch. 7 Building

_____

_____

For each name you put down in the above table, what are some ways you can intentionally invest in those relationships to meet your goal?

Name:	What You Plan to Do:

Great work! You've not only taken the time to identify a variety of relationships in your life, you've also intentionally identified friendships that you'd like to deepen, and you've named specific ways you plan to do so. You're well on your way to growing in these important relationships and helping others deeper friendships in the process!

> "There are no strangers here; only friends you haven't yet met."
> –William Butler Yeats

💡 Applied EI: After 30 days, return to these lists and your stated goals. How're they going? Have you seen any progress? Building relationships can take time, of course. So, even if you haven't seen much progress, be encouraged and stay the course. Keep being intentional.

Take time to make notes on ways you have tried to create deeper friendships. What worked? What didn't work?

_____

_____

_____

_____

_____

Ch. 7 Building

_____

_____

_____

If you're struggling to connect with someone on the list, give it some time, but allow for the fact that you can't get closer to everyone. Every relationship is a two way street!

SOCIAL SKILLS

Social skills are the necessary ingredient to create and maintain meaningful relationships. In the workplace and your personal life, social skills are the difference between relational success and failure. Dr. Daniel Goleman refers to social skills as the interpersonal aspect of Emotional Intelligence.

Having a high EI requires mastering certain social skills, sometimes called "soft skills." These include everything we do in our interactions with others: from active listening and reading nonverbal cues to speaking clearly and maintaining eye contact. Every interaction we have with other people is regulated by our soft skills.

Social Skills is a broad category of the ways we engage with others, but here are some helpful examples:

Maintain Eye Contact	*Speaking Up*	*Compassion*	*Teachability*
Accepting Criticism Well	*Remaining Positive*	*Patience*	*Honesty*
Proper Body Language	*Show Respect*	*Resilience*	*Active Listening*

Categorizing Social Skills: Seeing, Thinking, and Doing

Dr. Eileen Kennedy-Moore categorizes social skills in three ways: Seeing, Thinking, and Doing. "Seeing" social skills refers to monitoring others and picking up on social cues. This includes being able to read nonverbal cues and make the necessary adjustments to relate well to others. Can we notice when someone appears uninterested, or do we simply keep rambling on? Can we recognize when we're in a context that requires more formality and adjust our language accordingly? All this starts with seeing.

"Thinking" social skills involve interpreting other people's intentions from their behavior. This includes being able to tell the difference between someone acting deliberately to hurt us or accidentally offending and responding appropriately. Those who struggle with social skills often fail to interpret other people's actions or words and their misinterpretations lead to frustration or hurt.

Lastly, "Doing" social skills help us to act the way we intend and fits our context. If you're leading a meeting but struggle to speak up, that's a Doing failure. Likewise, if you need to remain silent and allow others to lead a meeting but keep interjecting, that, too, is a failure to act appropriately.

All of these three aspects of social skills—Seeing, Thinking, and Doing—are necessary for building meaningful relationships, and they are key aspects of Emotional Intelligence.

Self-Assessment:

How would you rate yourself when it comes to each of these social skills, on a scale from 1 to 10, where 1 is struggling with social skills, and 10 is excellent at social skills?

Low "Seeing" Social Skills　　　　　　　　　　**Excellent "Seeing" Social Skills**

1　2　3　4　5　6　7　8　9　10

Low "Thinking" Social Skills　　　　　　　　　**Excellent "Thinking" Social Skills**

1　2　3　4　5　6　7　8　9　10

Low "Doing" Social Skills　　　　　　　　　　**Excellent "Doing" Social Skills**

1　2　3　4　5　6　7　8　9　10

Using this self-assessment can be a helpful starting point for measuring your social skills. You can also take this online quiz (takes about 20 minutes):

www.psychologytoday.com/us/tests/relationships/social-skills-test

If you took the test, how'd you do? How'd your score on this *Psychology Today* test compare to your self-assessment?

_____

_____

_____

Referring to the above examples of social skills (seeing, thinking and doing), where would you like to improve?

_____

_____

_____

_____

Way to be honest—that takes intentional self-reflection and, at times, painful honesty.

Researchers agree that social skills are learned from others—*for better or for worse*! Who's a model of healthy social skills in your life? What social skills stand out when you think of them?

_____

_____

_____

Let's commit to improving your own social skills by modeling this person. What steps can you take in the next week to follow their example? Be as specific and actionable as possible:

_____

_____

_____

_____

_____
_____
_____
_____
_____
_____
_____

> "We're losing social skills, the human interaction skills, how to read a person's mood, to read their body language, how to be patient until the moment is right to make or press a point. Too much exclusive use of electronic information dehumanises what is a very, very important part of community life and living together."
>
> –Vincent Nichols

💡 **Applied EI:** Set a reminder for yourself to check in on your Social Skills Assessment in 30 days (use your phone if it's helpful). Thinking about the specific skills you've been working on, how are you doing? Have you seen improvement? Reflect on that now:

_____
_____
_____
_____
_____
_____

We all have areas of growth in terms of our social skills. Keep being intentional about identifying opportunities for improvement and checking in with yourself, making notes and adjustments where you need to. And, keep an eye out for new models. Remember, positive social skills are contagious (as are negative ones)—use that as an opportunity to learn!

Ch. 7 Building

NAILING YOUR FIRST IMPRESSION

Your first 27 seconds in a conversation can make or break a relationship. Some research shows that we make judgements about others in less than 30 seconds after meeting them. Other research suggests you only have seven seconds. In fact, seven in ten Americans responded that they form a first impression before the other person even speaks![1]

How are you at first impressions?

Some of us get anxious about meeting others for the first time, whereas others get excited. In *Connect through Emotional Intelligence*, I offered three ways to improve your first impression: Remembering Names, Maintaining Eye Contact, and Keeping It Light (Pages 119-124).

In addition to these three strategies for making a good impression, here are a few more:
- Do your homework ahead of time on the other person and prepare some talking points
- Dress appropriately
- Be confident in your positive qualities (remind yourself ahead of time if you need to!)
- Believe that other will like you (some research is shown that your expectations are one of the greatest predictors of the first impression that you'll make)
- Relax
- Be polite
- Mind your tone of voice
- Use your Active Listening skills
- Seek out commonalities
- Ask thoughtful questions that invite the other person to share
- Shows interest with your body language (smiling, leaning in, keeping an open posture)

The point of the ALAER approach is not simply to understand what others are sharing. It is to demonstrate to them that you understand. You'll likely respond in a way that affirms all of the ways you've been actively listening, understanding, and exploring.

Your response may very well include offering your personal wisdom, but it will most certainly be informed by all that you have learned throughout the course of the conversation at-hand.

---

[1] "Seven Seconds to Make a First Impression," Carol Kinsey Goman, Forbes, February 13, 2011, https://www.forbes.com/sites/carolkinseygoman/2011/02/13/seven-seconds-to-make-a-first-impression/

"This Is Exactly How Long You Have to Make a First Impression," Tyler Schmall, New York Post, December 14, 2018, https://nypost.com/2018/12/14/this-is-exactly-how-long-you-have-to-make-a-good-first-impression/

Most people spend far too much time worrying about what they're going to say. In fact, research has shown your words are, by far and away, the least important factor:

- 55% of first impressions are made by what others see of you.
- 38% is the way others hear your first words.
- 7% of first impressions are shaped by your actual words.[1]

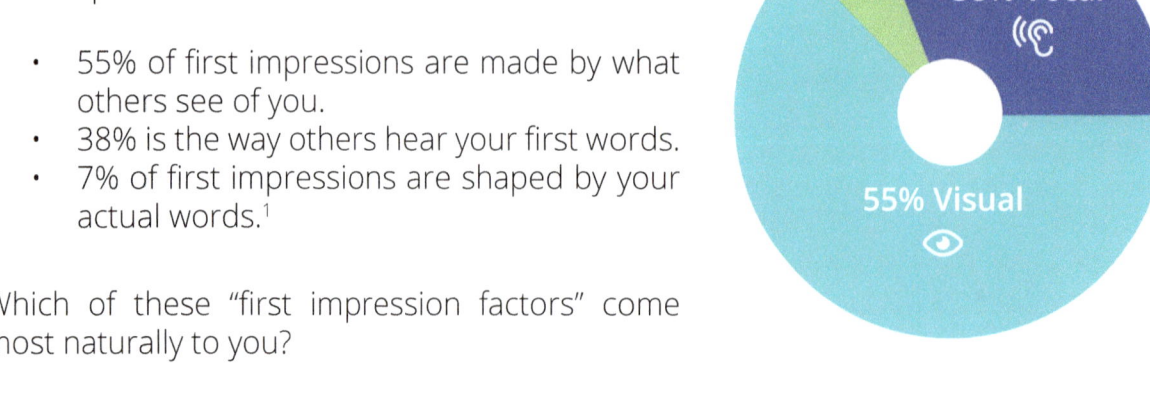

Which of these "first impression factors" come most naturally to you?

_____
_____

Which is the greatest opportunity for improvement?

_____
_____
_____

Reading Connect through Emotional Intelligence, were there any strategies that you found helpful and would like to try out for improvement here? If so, capture that now:

_____
_____
_____

Great! Now, what are some ways you can begin practicing this next week? Do you have a meeting where you'll be interacting with others for the first time? If not, can you set something up? Write that upcoming meeting down now, including the ways you can put this new strategy to use.

_____
_____

---

15   "What Makes a Good First Impression?" https://institute.uschamber.com/what-makes-a-good-first-impression/

> "What people say and feel about you when you've left a room is precisely your job while you are in it."
>
> –Rasheed Ogunlaru

 Applied EI: After preparing for this upcoming meeting, spend some time reflecting on how it went. What went well? What would you still like to improve on?

_____
_____
_____
_____

This level of intentional reflection is essential for seeing the kind of improvement you're after!

IMPROVING YOUR SOCIAL SKILLS: MINDFULNESS

Mindfulness helps us be fully present by paying attention to our thoughts and feelings—without judgement. We are constantly inundated with distracting thoughts and emotions that get in the way of our ability to be present and, hence, connect with others. Rather than ignoring what's bothering us and trying to "power through," Mindfulness invites us to notice when a feeling or thought arises, then name it, and then set it aside, allowing us to fully focus where we need to.

> "Mindfulness practice means that we commit fully in each moment to be present; inviting ourselves to interface with this moment in full awareness, with the intention to embody as best we can an orientation of calmness, mindfulness, and equanimity right here and right now."
>
> –Jon Kabat-Zinn

The Three Components of Mindfulness:

01	02	03
Noticing (your thoughts and emotions)	Labeling (without judgement)	Letting Go (so that you can be fully present)

Ultimately, Mindfulness comes down to just two things: Awareness and Acceptance. This is another tool to help you be fully present, which is key for improving your social skills, and necessary for building meaningful relationships with others.

Be honest, how do you feel about Mindfulness exercises?

_____
_____
_____

Is Mindfulness something you've practiced before? If yes, how did it go? If no, is there any reason?

_____
_____
_____
_____

💭 **Applied EI:** For the next 24 hours, give Mindfulness a try. When you notice a new emotion or feeling arise, don't ignore it. Actively identify it without any judgement about whether it was right or wrong to feel that way. Later, when you have time, return to that emotion. Why did you feel that way, at that moment? Did something happen to bring it about?

_____
_____
_____
_____

At the end of your day, reflect on how this went. Was this more difficult or easier than you imagined? Did you find it helpful? Why or why not?

_____
_____
_____
_____

If you found practicing Mindfulness helpful, add it to your toolbox! Use it every day as a way to be fully present, focusing on others in a way that improves your ability to build meaningful connections.

NONVERBAL COMMUNICATIONS

Being adept at nonverbal communications is key for building new relationships and having a high EI. We spent time in Chapter 4 covering the different aspects of nonverbal communications, and I gave you a chance to assess yourself. Now is a good time to return to that work. Remember, nonverbal communications include:

- Facial Expressions
- Physical Posture / Body Language
- Tone of Voice
- Distance (Close or Standoffish)
- Hand Gestures
- Eye Gaze
- Appearance

All of these nonverbal cues play an important role in your overall social skills and ability to make a strong first impression. This is true both for reading others and for practicing your own nonverbal communication skills.

Assessment: Reading & Practicing Nonverbal Communication
Having spent some time focusing on nonverbal communication, how would you evaluate yourself on reading nonverbal communications now?

Least Skilled   **Most Skilled**

① ② ③ ④ ⑤ ⑥ ⑦ ⑧ ⑨ ⑩

How'd this score compare to your results back in Chapter 4? Have you noticed improvement? If so, where?

_____
_____
_____

Now, how would you evaluate yourself on practicing these nonverbal communications to make a strong first impression?

Least Skilled   **Most Skilled**

1   2   3   4   5   6   7   8   9   10

Where would you like to improve on using nonverbal communications in order to nail your next first impression?

_____
_____
_____

If you have a meeting coming up, name three things that you plan to do to make a positive, lasting first impression:

1. _____

2. _____

3. _____

Return to this list afterward and make notes on how it went.

_____
_____
_____

Evaluating your performance with regular check-ins is a sure way to see improvement. Keep up the good work!

COMMUNICATION STYLES

In *Connect through Emotional Intelligence*, I introduced four communication styles, some better than others (Pages 128-131). Refer to these and study them before answering the following questions.

Describe each of the following communication styles in your own words. If you can, list an example of someone you know for each.

Aggressive Communication   **Example:**

_____

_____

Passive Communication   **Example:**

_____

_____

Passive-Aggressive Communication   **Example:**

_____

_____

Assertive Communication   **Example:**

_____

_____

Now, which of these communication styles best describes you? Note some specific examples. Are you happy with that answer?

_____
_____
_____
_____

In what ways would you like to be more Assertive in your communications? What challenges do you face and how can you overcome those hurdles?

_____
_____
_____
_____
_____
_____
_____
_____
_____
_____
_____
_____
_____
_____

Applied EI: In the next week, take note of the different communication styles you notice. Maybe it's in work meetings, or maybe it's at home. Pay special attention to those using Assertive Communications—and what you can learn from them. Being able to recognize these styles will help you navigate conversations and create strong connections.

Ch. 8 Maintaining

Chapter 8:
MAINTAINING

If you're old enough, you remember road trips prior to smartphones and GPS. "Just follow me," was a recipe for disaster. So much could go wrong. If the leader wasn't paying attention or if the follower got pulled over (because the leader was speeding), you might never make it to your destination. Moving from "them" to "us" takes more than one interaction. It requires building and maintaining a relationship and keeping the destination in sight.

What makes or breaks most friendships in your life? What's the difference between those that have lasted and those that have faded away? In my life, it's come down to one thing: Intentionality. Those with a high EI have an established and sturdy foundation of friendships that they've maintained and can call on to help navigate difficult times.

We cannot always be in touch with everyone. There are some phases of life that require us to be more focused on our work, for example, or our family. But the difference between the relationships that last and those that do not is intentional maintenance.

Once we have built meaningful relationships, the work doesn't stop. It simply shifts. It still take's intentional effort and work—being present with others when they need us, spending regular time together, and finding ways to help them manage their emotions.

We're going to explore each of these aspects of maintaining relationships, digging deeper into being present, spending regular time, and helping others manage their emotions. But, first, let's take some time to assess some of your most successful friendships and what has worked well for you.

What's one relationship in your life that has stood the test of time? Maybe it's overcoming distance, or an especially busy or difficult phase of life. What has been helpful in that friendship?

_____
_____
_____
_____

Who is someone in your life who has been intentional about investing in your friendship? What are some specific things they have done that have been helpful?

_____
_____
_____
_____
_____
_____

What are your preferred ways of staying in touch with friends? What is your least favorite? Most importantly, what has been the most effective?

Preferred: _____
_____
_____

Least favorite: _____
_____
_____

Most effective: _____
_____
_____

BEING PRESENT

Sometimes the best thing we can do for a friend is simply to be present with them. We may think they need us to solve their problems, but they may simply need to be reminded they're not alone.

Think of a trying time from your own life when someone was present with you in a helpful way. What did they do to show you that they were present?

_____
_____
_____
_____
_____
_____

Has there been a time when someone close to you went through a trying time and you struggled to be present with them? What made that so hard?

_____
_____
_____
_____
_____
_____

What are some helpful ways to tell the difference between when others need you to get involved and when they simply need you to be present?

_____
_____
_____
_____
_____

An Example of Being Present: Sitting Shiva

We can learn a lot about how to be present from the ancient Jewish practice of sitting shiva. This seven-day period allows those who are mourning to put a pause on life and experience their grief without responsibilities and distraction. It demonstrates our need for others to be present in our grief. Not to solve it, but to simply remind us that we are not alone.

Rabbi Ana Bonnheim offers the following reflections on what to say when visiting or calling someone sitting shiva[1] :

> *It is customary to wait to speak until after the mourner speaks. But, once you are acknowledged, all you need say is "I'm sorry." That simple phrase, a touch, or a hug will mean more to the mourner than you can ever know.*
>
> *Shiva is a time to reminisce, remember, and recapture memories of a loved one. As such, a focus of a condolence call is to listen to those memories that the mourner wishes to share or to talk about other subjects initiated by the mourner that may have nothing to do with his or her loss.*
>
> *Shiva condolence calls do not need to be longer than 30 minutes. Supporting, listening, and responding to the mourner are primary goals....*
> *Just being present is the main objective.*

Here are some important takeaways for us:
- Let them lead—don't feel you have to keep conversation going if they don't seem interested in talking.
- Don't feel like you have to come up with an explanation or a solution.
- If you feel the need to speak, keep it short. "I'm sorry" is sufficient.
- If they do feel like talking, put your active listening skills to work and let them guide where the conversation goes. This will help them feel heard and understood.
- Most importantly, remember: your presence is present enough!

---

17   "Everything You Need to Know About the Jewish Custom of Shiva," Rabbi Ana Bonnheim, https://reformjudaism.org/everything-you-need-know-about-jewish-custom-shiva
   "Friendships: Enrich Your Life and Improve Your Health," by Mayo Clinic Staff, https://www.mayoclinic.org/healthy-lifestyle/adult-health/in-depth/friendships/art-20044860

REGULAR TIME

Investing in friends is one way to invest in your health. Making regular time for good friendships is like getting regular physical exercise Friendship's health benefits include:

- Reduced rates of depression
- Lower blood pressure
- Reduced BMI (Body Mass Index)
- Longer life expectancy

Research also shows that those who regularly reach out to friends are more likely to have deeper friendships[1]. The Psychologist John Gottman used the term "bids" when referring to the ways couples make requests for contact with one another. But bids happen in friendships, too. In these relationships, more bids lead to more depth, vulnerability, and trust.

> "Adults with strong social support have a reduced risk of many significant health problems, including depression, high blood pressure and an unhealthy body mass index (BMI). Studies have even found that older adults with a rich social life are likely to live longer than their peers with fewer connections."
>
> –Mayo Clinic

But strong friendships don't just happen. They come through intentional, regular time together. Some friendships may go months or even years between talking. Still, somehow you're able to pick up right where you left off. But most relationships require regular time together, catching up on the phone, connecting over FaceTime, or spending time together in person. And this requires intentionality. It requires effort.

From Connect Through Emotional Intelligence, page 140

... maintaining relationships requires spending regular time together. Simply checking in, even when nothing special is going on, is a way of showing others that we care, and that they are important to us.

It Starts With a Plan

How we order our life determines the number and depth of our friendships. We may want to have deeper friendships, but if we're not ordering our life to prioritize regular time with friends, it's not going to happen. It requires a plan. It requires time. And it's worth the investment, paying rich dividends socially, physically, and emotionally!

Before we create a plan for maintaining and deepening them, let's spend some time thinking about the friendships in your life.

Who is the last friend that you spent time with, either on the phone or in-person? Is this someone you spend time with regularly? If so, how often? What has been helpful for making that happen?

_____
_____
_____
_____
_____
_____

Who are some of the other friends who you're in touch with most regularly? What has been helpful for doing so?

_____
_____
_____
_____
_____
_____

Who are the friends you haven't connected with recently, but you would like to?

_____
_____
_____

Creating regular time together can be a challenge, given busy work schedules, distance, or entering a new phase of life, but here are some ways to help you maintain the relationships that are important to you.

Create a Check-In Schedule

Like I shared in *Connect through Emotional Intelligence,* there was a time when I was so busy with a graduate program that I literally charted out my different relationships, creating a plan for staying in touch with each person to maintain our friendship. Here's a chart for you to use, identifying friends you want to stay in touch with on a weekly or monthly basis, when to check in, and how you'll do so.

As you fill this out, keep everyone's schedules in mind. Also be sensitive to their preferred means of connection. Some prefer a phone call over a virtual meeting. Others want to meet in person and others want to do something (as opposed to just talk). Keep the specific person in mind as you're planning how best to stay in touch.

> "You can make more friends in two months by becoming interested in other people than you can in two years by trying to get other people interested in you."
> –*Dale Carnegie*

Friends to Connect with Weekly:	When You Will Check In:	How:
_____	_____	_____
_____	_____	_____
_____	_____	_____
_____	_____	_____

Friends to Connect with Weekly:	When You Will Check In:	How:
_____	_____	_____
_____	_____	_____
_____	_____	_____
_____	_____	_____

Great work! Preparing an intentional plan will help you maintain regular time together and build closer relationships. Keep this plan handy and check in to make sure you're sticking with it.

Multiple Connections

Another thing to keep in mind is that the more types of connections we have with people, the more likely those relationships are to grow in depth. If you're only connecting with a colleague at work, for example, but you're wanting to invest in that friendship, consider other ways to connect outside of work—such as a book group, sharing a regular meal outside of work, or exercising together. Think about this as you're getting in touch. Offer new ideas on ways to connect to take the friendship deeper.

Set Reminders

If you're worried about making a plan and keeping it, set yourself reminders so that you don't drop the ball. Your phone's reminder tool is an easy solution. Creating a reoccurring reminder, either weekly or monthly, for each person will help you make sure you're keeping to your plan.

Use Meeting Apps

One of the challenges is that everyone's schedules are so full. Thankfully, there are a wide variety of tools and apps to help you coordinate schedules.

Here are just a few examples:
- When2Meet
- Acuity Scheduling
- Doodle
- Setmore

These are a few scheduling tools that I've found helpful. Try them out and see what works best for you!

> 💡 **Applied EI:** Set yourself a reminder to check in on your lists in 30 days. Are there friends that you've connected with more than once? Or are there friends that you're trying to connect with but it's just not working? If so, re-evaluate your check-in schedule, and how you're connecting. Do you need to try something different?
>
> If you try a few different approaches and it's still not working, then it might be time to take a break. Circle back again in a few weeks. In the meantime, celebrate what's working well, and the friends you've been able to connect with!

MANAGING OTHERS' EMOTIONS

How are you at helping others handle their emotions?

Those with a high EI can recognize the times when simply being present is not enough, and they are able to come alongside to help them respond to what others are going through. Knowing that is an essential part of having a high EI. The best approach? Identify (the concern) and Ask (if they'd like help).

"It looks like something is bothering you," you might say—the Identification. The ask, "Is that something you'd like to talk about?" or "Can I help?"—the Ask. In most cases, the other person will be able to let you know if they want help.

Another approach is using the ALAER approach from Chapter 6: Ask, Listen, Acknowledge, Explore, and Respond. But remember that Respond only comes in *after* the rest of the critical steps. Study this approach and put it into practice to help others when needed.

Now, let's think about some examples of when you've had help managing your emotions, or when you've helped someone else.

Learning By Example

Think about a time when you felt overwhelmed and needed help managing your emotions. Got one? If so, what was going on? What were you feeling?

_____
_____
_____
_____
_____

Can you think of someone who was able to help? What did they do that was helpful? Write that down now, being as specific as possible.

_____
_____
_____

Now, think about a time when someone you know needed help managing their emotions. What was happening?

Thinking of this example, what did you do that was helpful? What did you try that didn't go well?

Great work! Actively reflecting on what others have done for you and what you have done is a great way of identifying and building up this skill in your own life.

Chapter 9: SOLVING

Back to the road trip analogy. Thanks to everyone being responsible with their own cars, skillfully navigating the crowded freeway, and maintaining good communication with everyone else in the party, you all arrive safe and sound at the campground and start setting up the tents. But then the rain starts coming down. The person assigned to make the first dinner left their ice chest at home. The campground has run out of firewood. As you sit around an empty fire pit eating power bars for dinner, tempers begin to flare. You realized that what happens over the next couple days will either pull the group apart or else bring you all together.

When it comes to relationships, conflicts are inevitable. . Emotional Intelligence won't prevent conflicts. In fact, a lack of conflict can indicate a lack of relational depth. But it *can* help solve a problem before it becomes destructive.

Sooner or later, every relationship comes to a point where challenges must be addressed. Whether it's a friendship, a colleague, a family member, or otherwise, we all face issues with others that require a high EI to navigate well. EI can help solve a little problem before it becomes a big problem.

In this chapter, we will conclude with a series of social skills you need to navigate any number of issues you may face when connecting with others. We will talk about how to receive and reframe criticism. We will cover ways to successfully deliver hard feedback to ensure positive improvement. And I will give you the tools you need to effectively address and resolve conflict when it arises, helping ensure you're able to navigate to a healthy solution.

Ch. 8 Maintaining

Real Life Examples

To keep this conversation practical, I'd like you to think of some challenging situations you've recently faced or are currently facing. This may be an ongoing issue with someone you regularly interact with or a one-off event with a stranger. Whatever the case, take a few minutes to list out the individual involved and the conflict. Be sure to include specifics and show the issue from both individual's perspectives.

Before we create a plan for maintaining and deepening them, let's spend some time thinking about the friendships in your life.

Individual	Challenging Experience
1._____	_____
2._____	_____
3._____	_____

Great work! It's not easy to wade into challenging experiences. Most of us would rather avoid challenging experiences than return to them. But by reflecting on them, we can find ways to work through and learn from them.

Let's get started!

REFRAMING CRITICISM

Did you know your brain is hard-wired to notice and remember criticism more than compliments? It's called a negativity bias. "Almost everyone remembers negative things more strongly and in more detail," says Clifford Nass, a Communications Professor at Stanford

University[1]. For every one compliment you've received, you can probably name many more critiques. Research shows that this tendency is generally true across the board. It can be helpful to know, you're not alone!

One of the reasons is that we often interpret criticism as a threat. "Threats to our standing in the eyes of others are remarkably potent biologically, almost as those to our [physical] survival," Dr. Daniel Goleman writes. At the same time, age also plays a role in this trend. Folks in their twenties and thirties tend to fixate more on negative incidents, but the older we get, the easier it is to live in the present and focus more on positive experiences than negative.

Rather than feeling sunk or ashamed of criticism, those with a high EI are aware of their shortcomings and are actively working on addressing them as opportunities for growth. Reframing criticism as an opportunity for growth can make the difference between feeling defeated by critics and defeating them.

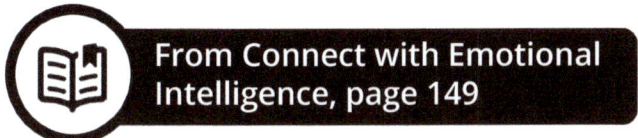
From Connect with Emotional Intelligence, page 149

When we know our own strengths and weaknesses, we are less likely to be surprised or offended when others bring up areas that we need to work on. Before we can respond to criticism from others in healthy ways, we must be able to identify areas for growth in our own life. Of course, it helps if we're already actively working on them.

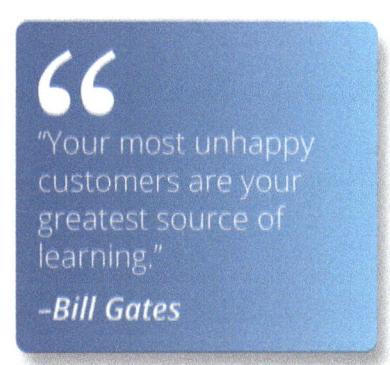
"Your most unhappy customers are your greatest source of learning."
–Bill Gates

Being aware of criticism, reframing it as an opportunity for growth, and then setting a plan for improvement. Let's practice that now.

What are three critiques that have gotten under your skin?

1. _____
2. _____
3. _____

Naming criticism you've received can be difficult, but it's the first step to overcoming it. Now, paraphrase each criticism, and name the personal growth opportunity you see in it.

Criticism   **Growth Opportunity**

1. _____   _____

2. _____   _____

3. _____   _____

Way to take these criticisms and turn them into an opportunity for improvement! Some of these issues are likely to be ingrained from years of habits. Some of them may be more recent. Still, none of them improve if you don't have a plan for addressing them. For each criticism, I'd like you to name one thing you can do to improve in this area.

Criticism   **Plan for Improvement**

1. _____   _____

2. _____   _____

3. _____   _____

Reframing criticisms as opportunities for growth is a way of establishing your own agency in these areas. Which is to say, naming and deliberately addressing the criticism takes the power away from your critics. And if the issue comes up again, you'll already have a plan in place to address it.

Then when a new criticism comes up, use the same practice—identify the opportunity for growth and set a plan for improvement. This approach is key not only to your own improvement, but also overcoming hard feedback rather than being overcome!

 "I think that's an important thing to do, to really pay attention to negative feedback, and solicit it, particularly from friends. This may sound like simple advice, but hardly anyone does that, and it's incredibly helpful."

—*Elon Musk*

⌬ Applied EI: In the next 30 days, notice whether these areas for improvement come up in conversation. If they do, how did you feel about it? Did you feel better knowing that you're already working on it? Or, do you get down on yourself for not having overcome it? Note the times when it came up and how you feel.

_____
_____
_____
_____

Keep putting in the work on each of these areas and, over time, you'll see improvement, feel proud of the work you put in, and be even more confident moving forward!

DELIVERING HARD FEEDBACK

"When I stop getting on to you, that's when you need to worry!" Have you ever heard that before? Maybe it was a coach in sports while growing up or a supervisor who seemed to give constant feedback. Whoever it was, their point was clear: hard feedback may be hard to hear, but it's the only way we get better.

High EI leaders know this and keep it in mind whenever they offer constructive criticism.

From Connect Through Emotional Intelligence, page 154

Just as receiving criticism is hard, so, too, is delivering it. Pointing out something that an employee needs to improve on can be so uncomfortable for some leaders that they avoid it and make the situation worse. Being able to offer critical feedback in a helpful way is a key mark of effective leaders.

How about you, how do you feel about delivering criticism? On a scale of 1 to 10, where 1 means you embrace it because it gives people an opportunity to grow and a 10 means you'd do anything to avoid it because it makes you uncomfortable, how would you rate yourself? (Note: If you really enjoy it you might be a bully, so give yourself a 0. Just kidding, but seriously, that's bad.)

How about you, how do you feel about delivering criticism? On a scale of 1 to 10, where 1 means you embrace it because it gives people an opportunity to grow and a 10 means you'd do anything to avoid it because it makes you uncomfortable, how would you rate yourself? (Note: If you really enjoy it you might be a bully, so give yourself a 0. Just kidding, but seriously, that's bad.)

Embrace It **Avoid It**

1　2　3　4　5　6　7　8　9　10

Is delivering hard feedback something you have room to improve in? In what ways?

_____
_____
_____

In Chapter 9 of *Connect through Emotional Intelligence*, I introduced several ways to help improve your delivery of hard feedback. Refer back to that chapter and, in your own words, provide a brief definition of each skill and an example of when you used it.

> "Feedback and respectful confrontation are gifts we share to help one another grow."
> —Frederic Laloux

Build Confidence

_____
_____
_____

Regular Compliments

_____
_____
_____

But vs. And

_____
_____
_____

Specific & Personal

_____
_____
_____

Critical Questions

_____
_____
_____

Collaborative Solutions

_____
_____
_____

Be Present

_____
_____
_____

Which of these skills would you most like to improve the next time you need to offer constructive criticism?

_____

Nice work recognizing which of these skills you'd like to practice. Also think about how you would like to adapt these skills to your own personality. Remember, those with a high EI always want to help others improve. Hard feedback is for their benefit—make that your goal!

RESOLVING CONFLICTS

Applied EI: The next time you have hard feedback to deliver, return to this chapter and put these skills into practice. Then, reflect on how it went. What worked well? What could still be improved?

_____
_____
_____
_____

Each time you practice delivering hard feedback, you will find it gets easier, and, more importantly, you're better you'll get at helping others improve. Keep at it!

When it comes to conflict, are you someone who digs in and engages, or are you more likely to retreat and disengage? Rate yourself on this scale:

Engage   **Disengage**

① ② ③ ④ ⑤ ⑥ ⑦ ⑧ ⑨ ⑩

Reflect on your score. Where do you think that comes from? Does your score reflect your personality? How does your family of origin shape your response?

_____
_____
_____
_____

Some of us have had helpful, healthy models of conflict. Others have not. But just because conflict happens, that doesn't mean it has to produce more hurt or harm. Conflict can be managed in healthy ways that prevent further harm and allow for mutual solutions. Those with a high EI know this. And they know how to respond to conflict when it comes up.

That's what we're going to work on in this section. Let's start with your own experience When was the last time you managed a conflict well? What did you do that was helpful? Was there anything the other person did that helped?

> "Conflict can and should be handled constructively; when it is, relationships benefit. Conflict avoidance is *not* the hallmark of a good relationship. On the contrary, it is a symptom of serious problems and of poor communication."
>
> –Harriet B. Braiker

When was the last time you were in a conflict that did not end well? What prevented you from finding resolution? In hindsight, is there anything that you could have done differently?

_____
_____
_____
_____

_____
_____
_____
_____

Practicing Conflict Resolution

Now that you've taken the time to think about positive and negative examples of conflict, let's use the three-step conflict resolution practice offered by Dr. Susan Heitler, explained in *Connect through Emotional Intelligence*:

01	02	03
Find the Source and Discuss Potential Solutions	Explore the Source of the Conflict	Determine a Mutual Solution

Returning to your three real-life examples from the start of this chapter, and pick one that you would like to process through these three steps.

01 Find the Source and Discuss Potential Solutions

What was the source of the conflict? And, what are some potential solutions? Try to answer this from the other person's perspective, as well as your own.

Source: _____

_____

_____

Potential Solutions: _____

_____

_____

02 Explore the Source of the Conflict

Now that you've identified the source of the conflict and potential solutions, let's spend more time digging into the source you identified. Here's where you lean into your curiosity.

What else can you learn about the underlying source? Sometimes, our first answer is only a surface-level issue. Were there any other, deeper factors that may have contributed? One technique is to ask, "If we were able to resolve the immediate cause, would there still be something else needing to be addressed?"

Ch. 8 Maintaining

_____
_____
_____
_____
_____
_____

03 Determine a Mutual Solution

Now that you've re-evaluated the initial source of the conflict and looked for the underlying cause(s), it's time to return to the initial solution in step #1. Does it need to be revised now? And, of course, ensure that the solution is mutually agreeable for both parties. To be successful, both parties must feel like they have been seen and heard.
Once you have a mutual solution in mind, write it out here.

_____
_____
_____
_____
_____
_____
_____
_____
_____
_____
_____
_____

> "If we manage conflict constructively, we harness its energy for creativity and development."
> –Kenneth Kaye

Great work applying these three steps to one of your own conflicts. This exercise can be helpful for imagining alternative responses, and for improving your response next time. Return to it anytime you need to work through a conflict.

Just as receiving criticism is hard, so, too, is delivering it. Pointing out something that an employee needs to improve on can be so uncomfortable for some leaders that they avoid it and make the situation worse. Being able to offer critical feedback in a helpful way is a key mark of effective leaders.

A FINAL CHECK-IN

Just as receiving criticism is hard, so, too, is delivering it. Pointing out something that an employee needs to improve on can be so uncomfortable for some leaders that they avoid it and make the situation worse. Being able to offer critical feedback in a helpful way is a key mark of effective leaders.

If you've made it this far, you've put in some serious reflection, planning, and practice, all aimed at improving your Emotional Intelligence. Great work! I am very proud of all that you've done to get to this point. I hope you see that it was time well spent.

In your own words, how would you now define Emotional Intelligence and describe the work you've done:

_____

_____

_____

_____

MEASURING YOUR SUCCESS

Now that you've completed the Connect through Emotional Intelligence workbook, take some time for one more intentional reflection. Here's a reminder of the different areas of EI that we've covered:

ME:	Them:	US:
Know Self	Identify	Building
Control Self	Empathize	Maintaining
Motivate Self	Explore	Solving

What are the three areas of EI where you're feeling most proud of?

1. _____
2. _____
3. _____

Where would you say is an area where you've seen the most improvement? What's made the difference?

_____
_____
_____

Great work in those areas! Now, what are the three areas of EI where you'd like to see more improvement?

1. _____
2. _____
3. _____

Now schedule one hour a week, for the next several weeks, to work on these areas and set a reminder on your phone. For the first week, return to the chapter for #1 above, and use the practices in this book to really drill in and focus on that area. The following week, move to the second area you identified. And then, for the third week, move to the third area. After that, either return to #1 or choose a new one and keep it going!

DON'T LOSE YOUR MOMENTUM!

After all of this work you've put in, you've built up some serious momentum for yourself. The worst thing you could do is to stop now. Create regular times for yourself to keep building on this work!

Remember, Emotional Intelligence is like a muscle. If you don't use it, it will atrophy. Committing yourself to continual improvement recognizes the importance of the work that you've put in—for yourself, and for others.

You've come so far already. Don't stop now.

Every interaction is an opportunity for practice and improvement. Every coffee meeting, every business meeting, every interaction at home—it's all an opportunity to build your EI and create deeper connections.

NEVER STOP GROWING!

In Connect through Emotional Intelligence, I tell the story of "Nick", an immensely talented salesman whose every success was shipwrecked by his inability to control his anger. Improving your EI is not about sitting in a circle and singing "Kumbaya." It is about becoming a fully functioning adult who enjoys a higher quality of life in every area—within themselves, in their home, with their friends, and in their workplace.

It is never too late to grow. Wherever your EI is now, it can be higher by this time next year—if you do the work. If you stay intentional. If you set reminders to check back in with yourself.

It will absolutely be worth it. It's not just me saying that. It's your co-workers, your friends, and your family.

So, please, keep up the good work!

SOURCES

Beck, Julie, "How Friends Become Closer," The Atlantic, August 29, 2017, https://www.theatlantic.com/health/archive/2017/08/how-friends-become-closer/538092/

Brand Genetics, "Empathy Statistics For Business," October 10, 2019, https://brandgenetics.com/empathy-statistics-for-business

Brown, Brene, "America's Crisis of Disconnection Runs Deeper Than Politics," Fast Company, September 12, 2017, https://www.fastcompany.com/40465644/brene-brown-americas-crisis-of-disconnection-runs-deeper-than-politics

Caren, Allie, The Washington Post, "Why we often remember the bad better than the good," November 1, 2018, https://www.washingtonpost.com/science/2018/11/01/why-we-often-remember-bad-better-than-good/

Cherry, Kendra, Very Well Mind, "Understanding Body Language and Facial Expressions," September 28, 2019, https://www.verywellmind.com/understand-body-language-and-facial-expressions-4147228

Emamzadeh, Arash, Psychology Today, "How Self-Esteem Changes Between the Ages of 4 and 94," September 11, 2018, https://www.psychologytoday.com/us/blog/finding-new-home/201809/how-self-esteem-changes-between-the-ages-4-and-94

Hartwell-Walker, Marie, PsychCentral, "How Many Friends Do You Need?" May 17, 2016, https://psychcentral.com/lib/how-many-friends-do-you-need

Jachimowicz, Jon M., Harvard Business Review, "3 Reasons It's So Hard to 'Follow Your Passions,'" October 15, 2019, https://hbr.org/2019/10/3-reasons-its-so-hard-to-follow-your-passion

Kennedy-Moore, Eileen, Psychology Today, "What Are Social Skills?" https://www.psychologytoday.com/us/blog/growing-friendships/201108/what-are-social-skills

Kinsey Goman, Carol, Forbes, "Seven Seconds to Make a First Impression," February 13, 2011, https://www.forbes.com/sites/carolkinseygoman/2011/02/13/seven-seconds-to-make-a-first-impression/

Konrath, Sara H., Greater Good Magazine, "What's the Matter With Empathy?" January 24, 2017, https://greatergood.berkeley.edu/article/item/whats_the_matter_with_empathy

Kraus, Michael, American Psychological Association, "Best Way to Recognize Emotions in Others: Listen," October 10, 2017

Levoy, Gregg, Psychology Today blog, "Novelty-Seeking: One of the Keys to Thriving in Life," April 19, 2018, https://www.psychologytoday.com/us/blog/passion/201804/novelty-seeking-one-the-keys-thriving-in-life

Mayo Clinic Staff, "Friendships: Enrich Your Life and Improve Your Health," https://www.mayoclinic.org/healthy-lifestyle/adult-health/in-depth/friendships/art-20044860

Miller, Michael, Six Seconds, "Seven Amazing Facts About Emotions You Should Know," https://www.6seconds.org/2018/02/19/7-amazing-facts-emotions/

Rabbi Ana Bonnheim, "Everything You Need to Know About the Jewish Custom of Shiva," https://reformjudaism.org/everything-you-need-know-about-jewish-custom-shiva

Schmall, Tyler, New York Post, "This Is Exactly How Long You Have to Make a First Impression," December 14, 2018, https://nypost.com/2018/12/14/this-is-exactly-how-long-you-have-to-make-a-good-first-impression/

Schumer, Lizz, The New York Times, "Why Following Your Passions is Good For You (and How to Get Started)," October 10, 2018, https://www.nytimes.com/2018/10/10/smarter-living/follow-your-passion-hobbies-jobs-self-care.html

Seiter, Courtney, Fast Company, "The Art And Science Of Giving And Receiving Criticism At Work," December 9, 2014, https://www.fastcompany.com/3039412/the-art-science-to-giving-and-receiving-criticism-at-work

ABOUT MIKE ACKER

Mike Acker is a keynote speaker, author, and executive and communication coach with over twenty years of experience in speaking, leadership development, and organizational management.

Known for his authenticity, humor, and engaging presence, Mike specializes in fostering personal and organizational awareness, allowing clients to create their own personal growth track. His approach is earnest, informed, and holistic, leading to a more satisfying balance in work and life. His expertise in communications and leadership has attracted politicians, business entrepreneurs, educational leaders, and executive managers.

Mike has been a professional speaker for over twenty years and has spoken to groups of 10 to 10,000. His training stretches from private Spanish schools in Mexico, to national college debate tournaments, master classes in cultural leadership, and certifications in coaching.

As a believer in giving back, Mike has worked with and supported several non-profits and relief organizations. Most recently, he served as the board chairman for GO on the Mission, an international non-profit working to lift kids out of poverty in Senegal and Mexico. (https://www.goonthemission.com.)

Mike also enjoys rock-climbing, wake surfing, skiing, church, building Legos with his son Paxton, and going on dates with his wife Taylor. Mike believes in the power of prayer, exercise, journaling, and real community to counter the stresses of everyday life.

www.mikeacker.com

Connect Through Emotional Intelligence

BOOK MIKE ACKER

FOR YOUR TEAM OR EVENT

Mike Acker is an in-demand keynote speaker on effective communication, emotional intelligence, and transformational leadership. His work in coaching, writing, and speaking inspires audiences around the nation and the globe. His first book, Speak With No Fear, achieved the status of the highest-ranking book on overcoming nervousness in speaking.

He has worked with Adobe, Amazon, Microsoft, Oracle, INOApps, Dallas International School, US Federal Agencies, International Monetary Fund, and many others.

If you are interested in booking Mike Acker for a keynote presentation, workshop, or virtual program, please contact info@mikeacker.com or visit www.MikeAcker.com.

Past Engagements Include:

Explore The Public Speaking School and work personally with Mike Acker:

1-on-1 Coaching

Professional Online Course Curriculum

Monthly Mastermind Cohort

Create Confidence through Communication.

1. Overcome insecurity and anxiety.
2. Learn how to connect with others.
3. Develop Executive Presence.

Don't wait: set up a free consultation:
https://advance.as.me/CTEI
(Available for individuals and teams)

ALSO BY MIKE ACKER

A **Lead with No Fear**
In this conversational and action-oriented book, Steve Gutzler and Mike Acker present seven shifts to direct your leadership towards your desired destination: impact, influence, and inspiration.

B **Speak with No Fear**
Speak With No Fear is the #1 globally highest-ranked book on overcoming the fear of speaking. Full of relatable anecdotes, executable tips, and plenty of laugh-out-loud moments, this book promises to teach you seven proven strategies to help you find your inner presenter.

C **Speak with Confidence**
Don't just overcome nervousness; discover Mike Acker's proven framework for developing profound confidence to eliminate self-doubt, second-guessing, and weak presence to excel in public speaking and succeed in life.

D **Write to Speak**
A simple guide to creating content that connects you with your audience. Readers will learn a repeatable system that works for novice and experienced speakers.

E **Connect through Emotional Intelligence**
In *Connect through Emotional Intelligence*, you will learn to master yourself, avoid disconnection with others, and bridge gaps through increasing your understanding and applying new principles. Increasing your emotional intelligence will improve your relationships, your leadership, and your life.

www.ingramcontent.com/pod-product-compliance
Lightning Source LLC
Chambersburg PA
CBHW061109070526
44579CB00012B/186